Saved from the Deepest Pit

To Bria, Morgan
and Cooper with
lots of love!
Uncle Scott, Aunt Kim,
JAYLE, ELISA!
Sidney!

Saved from the Deepest Pit

Billy Bray

Michael Bentley

CF4·K

10 9 8 7 6 5 4 3 2 1
© Copyright 2012
ISBN: 978-1-84550-788-6

Published by
Christian Focus Publications,
Geanies House, Fearn, Ross-shire,
IV20 1TW, Scotland, U.K.
www.christianfocus.com
email: info@christianfocus.com
Cover design by Daniel van Straaten
Illustrated by Brent Donoho
Printed and bound by Nørhaven, Denmark

NOTE: Much of the chapter entitled 'The Vicar is Saved' is based on Mr Haslam's own book, 'From Death into Life' by William Haslam, Tutis Digital Publishing Private Limited, 2008, pp. 39-41.

Contents

The Rock-fall

It was a long way down; a very long way indeed. Billy Bray sighed and took a fresh grip on the sides of the ladder as he resumed his descent into the darkness.

The daylight grew dimmer every time his foot felt for the next rung beneath him. Billy always missed the sunshine, but knew that if he did not work then he and his family would go hungry.

Although he had never been to school, Billy liked reading and he wondered what it might be like to be very rich and be able to go to a school.

As Billy started to go down yet another ladder he thought about poor Jim. The previous week, Jim had lost his footing and fell hundreds of feet to the rough ground at the foot of the ladders. Billy would never forget the look on the face of Jim's wife when he told her the awful news. As he continued his long downward journey, he wondered who would be the next miner to be seriously injured or killed.

'I want to think about more pleasant things,' he said to himself as he walked down yet another ladder. The only light now came from the candles stuck in the men's hats. Eventually Billy reached the bottom and started to walk to the end of a long tunnel where they would be working that day.

All was going well until suddenly there was a very loud noise. 'What's that?' screamed Billy, as he sprang up from his cramped position on the rock-strewn floor. At exactly the same moment his work-mate, Joseph, shouted, 'Be careful.' A fierce blast of scorching air hurled past them. The tiny flames on the candles suddenly shot out horizontally. For a moment, it seemed as if they would be left in complete darkness. They heaved a sigh of relief when they saw that their dim flames were still alight.

The two men could barely speak because they were coughing and spluttering so hard. Hundreds, or even thousands of tiny chips of rock must have shot past them.

Billy opened his mouth again, but before he could speak a low rumble came from further down the shadowy passageway. The sound gathered in intensity. The two men pressed themselves back against the rock. Just when they thought their ears would burst, the noise ceased with an enormous scream that echoed around the cavity where they were squatting.

Joseph stared at Billy, waiting to see how he would react to the rock-fall. Billy was well-known for making light of danger. Sometimes he used very rude words. His work-mates used to say, 'Billy laughs at danger. Nothing worries him.'

On this occasion, the look on Billy's face was quite different from anything Joseph had ever seen before. This time there was no light-hearted comment. Instead he muttered, 'We could have been goners if we'd stayed where we were.'

Thousands of tons of rocks had fallen in the very place where they had both been hacking away only a moment before the explosion.

Billy shuddered as he realised he could now be lying lifeless under an enormous weight of rock.

Today nothing light-hearted came from his lips.

Eventually Billy and Joseph's shift came to an end spurred on by the thought that today was pay-day. Billy made his way up the ladder as quickly as he could. Billy was eager to discover how much money he had earned.

Eventually, he saw dim daylight peeping through the tiny hole at the top of the shaft. Billy's thought turned to the ale house and the pint of beer waiting for him there. The meagre wages he earned were often spent on alcohol before they were ever spent on food for his wife and children.

The long climb to the surface had left all of the men longing for liquid refreshment. The owners of the bar knew this so they placed it just outside the mine manager's office. As Billy went into the room he noticed that many of his mates were already sipping their beer. He was not a patient man and he became even more edgy as he waited to be served.

Eventually, he had his drink and was sitting down with his friends.

People always enjoyed listening to Billy's wise-cracks, but then something very strange happened to him; his mind went completely blank. He normally had no problem thinking of something witty to say to make the men laugh, but this day nothing came. The men always looked for Billy to cheer them up when they were sad. They knew they could rely on him to entertain them with a joke – often at someone else's expense. A hush came over the room as the men waited expectantly.

Everyone looked in Billy's direction. Strangely, for the first time since he had begun working in the mines, Billy could think of nothing amusing to say. The only thing that came to his mind was a picture of his own broken body lying dead, crushed under the weight of that rock-fall.

He paused, and all his friends continued to stare in his direction. He opened his mouth and then he smiled as a new thought came to him. 'Wouldn't Dad be proud of me now, with all these men waiting to hear what I have to say?' He glanced down at the mug and picked it up again. While it was still halfway between the table and his mouth, another thought came to him. 'Would his dad really approve of him spending most of his hard-earned money on drink, and wasting his precious time with these coarse men?'

As these thoughts went round and round in his head, Billy realised how much he missed his father. It only seemed like a few days ago that he saw him last. Yet it was sixteen years since his death. Billy had only been seven.

The rest of the men may have wondered why Billy was so quiet but, then, from near the back of the room he heard whispered the words 'rock-fall' and he knew they had been told of their last-minute escape from death. The mood in the ale house gradually altered as the men grasped the horror of that situation.

Billy sighed and let his thoughts travel back over the years.

He had worked hard since he had left home when he was seventeen years old, but sadly many of his rare moments of relaxation had been spent in the bar.

He remembered the humble cottage where he had been born twenty-three years before. Did the roof still leak when it rained? Every other worker's house in the tiny village of Twelveheads had had a leaking roof.

His childhood had been happy, until the day his father died.

He found it difficult to understand why God should allow his wonderfully kind father to die. One day his dad had been at work down the mines with the rest of them, but when he came home he did not want any dinner and he staggered up to his bed. Soon after that his mother started to cry and the people from the other houses came in, and they cried too. Before long, some men came and took his daddy away. Billy saw his father's coffin being lowered into a hole in the church yard. When they covered it over with earth, he stood and cried.

Because his father was no longer there to earn money, it was decided that Billy should move to his grandfather's home, which was just down the lane.

The days spent with his grandfather were the happiest in his life. His grandfather taught Billy to love books and enjoy singing. Every Sunday, and sometimes during the week as well, they went to the Methodist Chapel in the village. His grandfather told him how he and some others had built it many years before.

A sense of pleasure flooded through Billy as he thought about those evenings when he had sat with his head in a book – in the book, the Word of God. The Bible was one of the few volumes in his grandfather's house and Billy read it over and over again. He loved all those stories about Jesus and the apostles, but most of all he liked the one about David and Goliath, the giant.

Billy loved to hear about the time when his grandfather visited Gwennap Pit when he was a young man. The pit was an old disused mine that had left a deep hole in the ground. Steps had been cut into the soil all the way around it. It looked a bit like a Roman amphitheatre. The steps made good places for people to sit and listen to a speech or a play. Because of its shape voices would be amplified and heard a very long way away.

Grandfather had heard that the Reverend John Wesley was visiting the area.

John Wesley travelled all around England to preach the good news of salvation and Jesus Christ. He spoke wherever people would listen to him. Some clergymen did not allow him to preach in their churches so John gathered the people around him and preached in the open air.

Billy remembered his grandfather had told him about that day, in 1762, when he had walked the few miles to Gwennap. Hundreds of other people were there as Mr Wesley spoke to them in that hollow pit.

Billy's granddad was born again that day. God spoke through John Wesley's lively preaching. He heard the call to repent of his sins and find peace by believing in Jesus.

Wesley spoke of how everyone was a sinner in need of God's forgiveness. The same message was told to the wealthy people who had studied at the big colleges in Oxford and the men who slept off the effects of their alcoholic drinks by the sides of the road.

Grandfather's old eyes had grown troubled as he told Billy how Mr Wesley had spoken about the terrible place called 'hell' where sinners ended up unless they repented and turned to Christ.

Then Mr Wesley explained the good news of the gospel. He told them that 'Jesus is alive today and everyone who is truly sorry for their sins may bring them to the Lord and he would take them away.' Mr Wesley explained that was why Jesus had died on the cross. 'He is the Son of God, the only one to live a sinless life. That meant that he was the only one who could give his life to pay for our sin.'

That day granddad and hundreds of others knelt down and called out to Jesus to wash them from their sins. Granddad had told Billy that this experience was being born again.

With a start, Billy suddenly remembered where he was. He looked at the mug of beer that was still in his hand and muttered to himself, 'Why didn't I follow granddad's advice?'

Instead of following his grandfather's way of life, he had gone in the opposite direction. Seeking fame and fortune were more valuable to Billy than following the teaching of Jesus.

The Desire for a New Life

Billy stared straight ahead of him. As a child his hands
had been soft and white, but now they were hard
because the jagged pieces of rock and sharp pieces
of metal from the wagons had torn into them. As
a young lad he had thought it was exciting to push
the big carts full of ore. His job was to take them to
the place where the men smashed them to pieces to
discover the thin strips of tin that ran through them.
The boys and girls who worked hard at this all day
earned just a few pennies. Billy had continued to do
these fairly simple jobs for a few years until the day
finally came when he was allowed to climb down the
steep ladders into the very depth of the mine.

There were periods in Billy's life when he had no
work. This meant that he had no money and he had
gone hungry. Then he remembered the relief he felt
every time he heard about a new mine being opened.
They always needed experienced workers.

When he had been seventeen, Billy had thought
that there must be more thrilling things to do than
working at the mines. Like many of his friends, he
longed to be free of the routine and solitude of West
Cornwall.

Billy remembered the day he spoke to his friend Jamie who had found a fresh life over the border in Devonshire. That conversation was what made Billy want to leave home. He longed to escape the routine of Twelveheads. 'There must be more things to do than going to chapel twice or three times on Sundays,' he muttered to himself. 'I'm bored with the class meetings on week evenings and I get so hungry when grandfather says very long prayers before we eat breakfast.'

It was soon after his seventeenth birthday when he said goodbye to his grandfather, and his other relatives in the village. He was on his way to his great adventure.

At first the days were happy and he sang to himself as he trudged along. Billy grinned as he thought about that time when he was sleeping under a spreading hedge and opened his eyes to see a rat staring into his face. He studied the animal intently until it shuffled up closer to him. He became worried when it started to sniff his nose. It was then that he jumped up and hurried onward. Leaving the little hamlet of Twelveheads certainly led to excitement, but it was not always of the most pleasant kind.

Often the footpath to Devonshire was hard to find and even when he was on the main roads he sometimes found them to be rough and boggy. Weary, hungry and tired Billy finally reached the northern border of Cornwall. He remembered thinking, 'I wonder what awaits me over there.' In the end he plucked up courage and crossed over into the next county. A strange new chapter was beginning in his life.

Life in Devonshire was as hard as it was in Cornwall. Billy eventually found work in a mine. However, tin mining in Devonshire was no easier than it was in Cornwall.

Even though he was in another county he quickly settled into his new life – and made many friends. One of his special friends was called Justin Thomas. How they enjoyed themselves in their spare time, and what good drinking partners they were for each other. When pay-day came around they would both spend many hours in the drinking house. It was there that Billy's strong voice often filled the place as he sang some of the old songs he had learned as a boy. Although some were traditional songs, others were very rude and they made the other drinkers laugh as they staggered around in their drunken stupors.

Billy's mind returned to the present as he looked down at his beer. It was still there. His mind may have been back in Devonshire but his body was still sitting at the table in Cornwall. As he looked at the head on the top of his drink, he began to realise that this liquid did not always bring happiness. It was certainly true in those Devonshire days. When he was seventeen he thought that if he drunk a great deal then he would be happy. He asked himself why people thought they were happy when they were filled with beer and he wondered whether it would be possible to be happy without being drunk.

Billy realised he was getting a bit morbid by thinking such things so he looked back again to those Devonshire days. There was that night when he and his friend Justin had been walking back to their home in an inn at Tavistock. They were thrilled to receive a much larger pay-packet than usual, so they spent much of it on beer. He almost laughed out loud when he remembered the horse. It was the horse, the very large horse that caused the problem. In the darkness they saw it looming up in front of them. Suddenly he had said, 'Do you want a ride Justin?'

'I think I'd better,' said Justin, 'because the beer that I have drunk makes it very difficult to stand up straight; perhaps the ride will make things easier.'

Billy smiled to himself as he recalled the great effort his friend had made to get up on the horse's back; but he soon fell off again and lay there, in the wet mud. Billy had done better because he had swung his leg up over the top of it and sat on it, although he quickly started to sway from side to side. Eventually, he managed to stay upright. He stretched down and grabbed Justin's hand. There followed a lot more laughter and chuckling, but eventually they were both sitting on the horse just before it started to amble away.

'See if you can get him to run faster,' said Justin from behind.

'I'm trying to,' said Billy, 'but the silly beast won't get into a gallop.'

At first they made steady progress but, without any warning the animal's foot struck a large stone which was sticking out of the ground. The horse stumbled a little, regained its balance but finally toppled over with a loud thud. 'Ow,' yelled Billy, 'it's sitting on top of me.' With great effort he managed to pull himself out from under the animal and they both staggered off into the darkness.

Eventually, they stumbled their way back to their lodgings and slept off the effect of the drink.

At the time, Billy had thought little of it, but they had been in danger that night. Thankfully, neither man had been injured. Today's amazing escape from the rock-fall made Billy realise that several times he had been saved from death. Perhaps God had been watching over him even then.

Billy began to feel ashamed of the wicked things that he had done in his youth. There was that time when he had been drinking heavily and had got into a fight with one of the other lads. It was late at night and an open fire burned in the clearing where they were sitting. He had hit the other lad several times but, because of his drink-ridden mind he had not noticed the fist of his opponent was heading straight for his head. He heard the crack as it smashed into his skull, and then felt the pain. It was a searing bang that forced his head backwards and he nearly lost his balance.

Even in his drunken state, he regained his balance quickly and then sat down while his opponent slinked away into the darkness. 'That was a close one,' he told himself, as he brushed down his clothes and put his hand up to adjust his miner's hat. Then he realised his hat was missing. 'My hat, where's my hat?' he shouted. And then he saw it. It was in front of where he had been sitting and it was resting between two flaming sticks in the fire. He got up to snatch it out, but it was so badly burned that it fell apart the second he grabbed it.

Billy's hat was an essential part of his equipment. Without it he would be unable to work. They were not just any hats; they were designed to hold a candle at the front of them. Without the light of a candle no miner could work. Panic seized him and then he saw the answer to his problem. Lying on the ground, quite close to him was someone else's hat. Billy rapidly shot out his hand and snatched it away. As everyone was now too much the worse for the drink, he was able to slink away under the cover of darkness. When he arrived back at his lodgings, he heaved a sigh of relief. He had got away with it. No one had seen him take it.

But he was wrong. The next morning he was rudely awoken by the arrival of the constable. 'You were seen stealing a miner's hat last night.'

'I never did,' said Billy. 'It must have been someone else because I have my own hat. Look, here it is!'

Billy and Justin had to move to a different district after that. And when Billy's temper got the better of him, they had to move on again.

They soon obtained work, and discovered somewhere reasonably comfortable to lodge. It was over a beer hall. Sleeping there meant they could quickly get a drink. Billy drank far too much of the powerful liquid and eventually he realised he was addicted to it. He reached the point where he spent every spare penny on alcohol.

Eventually Billy returned to Cornwall where he met a young woman named Joey. They got married and soon Mr and Mrs Bray had a growing family to look after. As he sat in the bar that evening, he was reminded that he soon ought to be going home to see them.

Joey had not been his first girlfriend and he was ashamed when he remembered his wicked life in the north. Now that he was a married man, that kind of life-style was in the past. Life with Joey was satisfying. It was good for him, but he wondered whether it was good for Joey. 'Why has the drink got such a hold on me?' he asked himself. He remembered, with shame, the time he had gone to buy coal for the fire and had called in at the ale house and spent the money on beer instead. He was so glad that she was a good and dutiful wife and had forgiven him for wasting so much money on drink. However, he felt ashamed when Joey had to fetch the coal and wheel it home because the drink inside him had made him fall over.

Once he had received two whole months' wages – £10 and he had given half of it to the local publican.

It provided many days of drinking for him. Pangs of conscience started to hit him as he remembered that Joey had to manage to run the household and buy food from the other £5, and she had to make it last for several months.

Billy then realised that he had stayed too long in the ale house. He loved his wife and he knew that she would be waiting for him. Perhaps some of the children would still be awake when he got home.

'I'm going now,' he called out to the others.

As he started to leave one of the men shouted, 'You haven't drunk your beer yet.'

For the first time in many years Billy had no taste for alcohol and he muttered, 'You can have it.'

With none of his usual cheeriness he mumbled, 'Good night,' and set off into the darkness.

The Beginning of a New Life

Something very strange began to happen to Billy as he walked home that night. He had a weird feeling that he was leaving his old life behind him and he was heading into something new. He had no idea what this meant, but he knew he had to go away from the beer hall in a hurry; he felt as though he was running away from the devil. For the first time in his life, Billy experienced a strange emptiness.

As he walked along Billy usually sang to himself, but this evening no music came. 'What is the most important thing in my life?' he asked himself. Certainly his work in the mine took up a lot of time, but was that really what gave his life meaning? No, his real life was at home. Even though the cottage was humble, and the roof and windows had been repaired many times, he was content with it. He worked hard in his garden. Some years he had a good crop of potatoes – enough to feed the family. Occasionally, there had even been produce over and he sold it to his neighbours. However, for some unknown reason tonight he could no longer say he was truly happy. Something was missing, but he was not sure what it was.

Billy thought about his grandfather. He had known what real happiness was, yet his life had been even harder than Billy's. Billy thanked God that his life was considerably easier than his granddad's had been.

At the top of the next hill Billy suddenly came to a stop. Why did he say that he thanked God? He had not thought about the Lord for many years.

Billy's mind went back to his mother. She still lived nearby and he visited her from time to time. He wondered whether she was happy.

As he plodded along, the same thought came into his mind over and over again. 'What is missing from my life?' As he puzzled over that, it suddenly came to him that he could not remember a pay-day when he had walked home without staggering from side to side. Today, he had drunk no alcohol at all and pretty much every penny of his earnings was safely in his pocket.

Joey was waiting as he approached the house. A puzzled look spread over her face. 'Are you all right Billy?' she said.

'Yes,' he replied, 'I stayed for a little while with the others, but somehow I didn't fancy my beer this evening.' He explained that he had no idea what was wrong with him, but he felt somehow different.

Without saying another word, Billy climbed the narrow stairs and laid his weary body on the old iron bed. Joey was worried. Billy usually treated her badly when he was drunk. On the other hand, he was a good and caring husband, especially when he was sober. She wanted to pray to God for help, but she had lost the habit of such things. She had not been to church very often since her childhood days. When she was quite young, she had asked the Lord Jesus to come and take control of her life but now, with all the work of running a household, she had almost forgotten him. 'I wish I hadn't wandered from the faith,' she mused. 'Billy could do with some prayer just now.'

Upstairs her husband was stretched out upon their bed, but sleep escaped him. He too, would have liked to have prayed but, even though there was no one else in the room, he felt unable to get out of bed and kneel down by the bedside. All he could think about was how his granddad had told him that Mr Wesley encouraged his people to read good books. Billy remembered that book he had read the other day. He did not know where it had come from, but it had been on a shelf in the kitchen. For the whole of the past week he had sat with his head in that book every moment he was free.

The first half was about heaven and the joys of eternal life. He wanted to go there one day, yet he hoped that it would not happen for many years.

He then remembered the name of the book. It had been written by Mr John Bunyan and was called, *Visions of Heaven and Visions of Hell*.

Still on the bed upstairs, Billy then thought about the second half of the book; the part about hell; the bit that scared him. What especially terrified him was

Mr Bunyan's story of two characters in hell. On earth they had been great friends, but in hell they shouted curses at the other for sending them there. 'I would never have been in this terrible place had it not been for my friendship with you,' one of the characters said.

His friend replied, 'And I would never have been in this terrible place had it not been for my friendship with you.'

Those words, 'my friendship with you,' shot round and round Billy's troubled mind as he lay in his restless state upon the bed. He knew it was only a story, but was it? What would happen if it was true and he ended up in hell? How would he feel if one of his friends were next to him in that dreadful place and they accused him of leading them astray?

As he thought about this, Sam Coad's face came into his mind's eye. He liked Sam very much and they had often worked together down the mine. They had drunk with each other too, and had often staggered home hand in hand. He thought, 'what if Sam and I ended up in the sufferings of hell together! My suffering would be made even worse if it was my bad behaviour that led him to be there too.'

He remembered the previous day when he was sitting at the end of the long table in his living room. He felt the heat of the fire upon his legs, but the warmth no longer held comfort. As he thought about it, the flames turned into the raging furnace of hell, a hell that burned on forever.

He wished that old Mr Bunyan had only written the first section of the book.

He knew that he needed to ask God to forgive his many sins. He had gone to bed straight from work because he was too ashamed to fall on his knees in front of Joey. As he lay there, he thought of those two friends in hell and he realised that his life-style could only be leading him to such an end. He did not have the joy that forgiven sinners knew.

Eventually, worn out and anxious, Billy drifted off into a thin, unsatisfying sleep. He was aware that later on Joey had slipped into bed beside him, but he did not move. He stayed that way until three o'clock in the morning. Then he could stand it no longer. He sat up in bed as carefully as possible because he did not want to disturb his wife. He knew he had to do something, and do so urgently. There was nothing else for it; he had to pray.

He quietly fell on his knees and tried to seek the Lord, but he had forgotten what to do since it was many years ago that he had last said his prayers. He was glad it was dark, so Joey could not see him as he cried out to the Lord to set him free from the power of sin. He knew that he could not release himself from its evil grasp. Even though he tried hard to pray, nothing happened; he still had no peace.

The next morning he stayed in his room. His sins were as heavy as the tons of rock that nearly buried him the day before. He longed to experience the freedom that his grandfather knew. Despite Joey's pleas for him to go downstairs and eat some breakfast, he stayed in the room and attempted to pour out his heart in prayer.

Eventually, Billy made a decision and came down the stairs. 'I'm going out,' was all he said to Joey as he staggered away into the chilly November air.

The Struggle for Happiness

Billy could never walk anywhere without being noticed. Children would shout to one another, 'Here's old Billy. Listen to him singing!' Whenever he was out walking, the hills and valleys reverberated with his voice. It might seem a strange thing to say, but his rather bad singing cheered everyone up. They all liked meeting, 'the man who had no cares in the world'.

But today things were very different. Billy made little sound as he wandered along. Those who passed by him noticed an anxious look was clouding his face. He looked like he had been awake all night.

He tried to concentrate on what he was doing and was sufficiently wide awake to realise that the ground was slippery with mud. He certainly knew that he needed to be careful where he placed his feet. Just then he saw a familiar tree by a fork in the path. Billy realised he was walking in the direction of the ale-house, but he no longer wanted to go in. Billy had changed. Once he had been the life and soul of the party. His mates called him 'chairman' as he was in charge of most of the fun and games in the bar.

His friends especially liked it when he made fun of the church and God or when he sang his rude songs or joined in a drinking contest. Seeing the ale in their mugs almost caused him to burst into tears as he thought of the trouble he had brought to his dear wife and children through his drunkenness.

When he passed the pub, one of his pals called out to him, 'Come away in Billy.' But Billy refused. The man swore an oath to which Billy replied, 'We must give an account for that kind of language one day.'

As Billy headed in the opposite direction, one of the drinkers said, 'Oh dear, it seems that we've lost our chairman!'

Joey was surprised to hear the sound of her husband's feet coming back so soon. She was even more startled to notice that he was sober. Before she could say anything he told her, 'You will never see me drunk again if the Lord helps me to resist the temptation.' Without another word he sat down at the table and ate the supper which she had hastily prepared for him. After his meal, Billy went upstairs, closed the door of the bedroom and fell down on his knees. He tried to remember how to pray. He did not know how to start and he felt so miserable that all he could do was call out, 'Lord, help me. You know that I'm a great sinner, but I do want to change.'

He wondered whether he was using the correct language and he hoped God would not mind. He just spoke to the Lord as he would talk to his mates – but without any swear words. He did not know how long he stayed on his knees, but he later became aware that

Joey had quietly entered the room to get ready for bed. He no longer felt embarrassed that Joey saw him on his knees. He finally stood up and climbed into his side of the bed. Whether it was his lack of sleep, or the fact that he had no more prayers inside of him, he did not know – he just kissed his wife 'goodnight' and they both fell into a deep sleep.

The next day was Saturday and after breakfast Billy took the family Bible and Wesley's hymn book and went up to the bedroom; these volumes had been untouched for many years. If he had no work on a Saturday morning, he would work in his small garden. Today he had more important things to do. He went to the only private place in the house – the bedroom.

He sat on the bed and started to read Psalm 23, 'The Lord is my shepherd, I shall not be in want.' As he did so, a puzzled look spread over his face. He knew that other people were comforted by those words, but they did nothing for him. He wondered whether the Lord Jesus was his Shepherd. He had always thought that religion was for older people, and seeking the Lord would be easy.

That Psalm worried him. He asked himself, 'Is the Lord my shepherd?' He became increasingly troubled and then he started to plead with God to tell him whether he was one of God's sheep. The Psalmist wrote, 'I will fear no evil,' but Billy did fear evil. Many times recently he had felt as though he was walking through the valley of the shadow of death. Billy was scared that he would end up in that dreadful place described by Mr Bunyan as hell.

Just then Billy opened the hymn book and read the first line of one of Mr Wesley's hymns, 'Weary souls that wander wide from the central point of bliss.'[1] He realised that he had never thought of the Lord Jesus Christ as the central point of bliss, and he certainly knew that he had been wandering far off from Jesus.

Billy came to the conclusion that there was no point in his life. But if that was true, why did God save him from that rock-fall? He noticed the next lines of the hymn and the words pierced deeply into his soul. 'Turn to Jesus crucified. Fly to those dear wounds of his; sink into the cleansing flood; rise into the life of God.'

Billy sank down on his knees again and actually shouted out to God, 'I want to turn to Jesus. I know he was hung up on a cross and crucified, but how can I be sure that he did that for me?' Then, in a much more quiet tone, he added, 'I'm not worthy of his love. My soul is in torment and I can find no purpose in life.'

Just then, Billy turned the page and read the second verse of the hymn, 'Find in Christ the way of peace, peace unspeakable, unknown; by his pain he gives you ease, life by his expiring groan.' Those words shouted out of the page into his soul. They drove him to prayer once again and he asked the Lord, 'Do you mean that it is possible to find peace, Lord?' He knew that there

---

[1] Hymn No. 319 in the Methodist Hymn Book 1933 edition.

was no peace in his heart. He was undeserving of any blessing from God.

His eyes drifted to the next two lines. It seemed as if God himself was calling them out to Billy, 'Rise, exalted by his fall; find in Christ your all in all.'

He wondered how he could find Christ. Tears filled Billy's eyes as he read the final verse, 'O believe the record true; God to you his Son hath given. You may now be happy too. Find on earth the life of heaven, Live the life of heaven above, all the life of glorious love.'

'I may be happy?' asked Billy. Then he realised that Mr Wesley meant that he, even Billy the tin miner could be happy. Happiness! That is what had filled his grandfather's life. If granddad and Mr Wesley knew that joy, then couldn't Billy find it too?

Later, a long while later, he went downstairs. He sat at the table and ate some of the food that Joey had prepared. She was a wise wife and did not ask too many questions. She could see that he was looking for something. Billy suddenly turned and reached out to his wife as he had before, 'O Joey, you once knew the peace of God and the happiness of trusting in Jesus, didn't you? Why don't you go back and find it again? If you did then perhaps I could have that happiness too.'

Joey looked at him and smiled a strange, contented smile. She did not like to see her husband so troubled, but she had a strange sense that something good, something marvellous, would soon happen.

Joey's mother called on them while Billy was having his dinner. She sat down next to her son-in-law and said, 'Joey tells me that you are seeking the Lord. I'm glad of that and I don't want you to give up seeking, but it may take you twelve months of hard work.' Billy looked sadly at her and almost shouted at her, 'It won't be as long as that before I find peace with God.'

'I'm going to bed,' he muttered and returned upstairs. As he knelt by his bedside his own words burned deeply into his soul. 'What will I do if I remain in this useless state for a whole year?' Suddenly his old confident self came back and he muttered, 'I will find peace, and I will find it soon.' As soon as he said that he was aware of a new voice, a terrible one. He did not know whether it was spoken out loud, or in his mind. It seemed as though it was coming from somewhere below him and in a cold voice it said, 'You will NEVER find God.'

He was puzzled. Who was speaking? Would the Lord say such a thing? Then he remembered what Mr Wesley had written in many of his hymns. He opened the tiny volume again and flicked through the pages. Everywhere his eyes went, he was urged to seek the Lord. Here was another one. It said, 'Come, all souls by sin oppressed.'[2]

'That's certainly me,' thought Billy. 'I've been selfish and blasphemed the name of the Lord, and I've

---

[2] Hymn No. 323 in the same book.

done it so often. Doubt entered his troubled mind again and he asked, 'Can God forgive someone as bad as me?' Then he wondered why Mr Wesley wrote these next lines, 'Ye restless wanderers after rest, ye poor, and maimed, and halt, and blind, in Christ a hearty welcome find.'

He knew he was 'a restless wanderer'. 'Would the Lord give me a hearty welcome?' He concluded, 'I don't think so. I have behaved too badly. If the Lord was to forgive me I would have to do many good works before my bad deeds could be washed away.'

As he thought about the impossibility of God's forgiveness he heard that unpleasant voice again. 'You will NEVER find God.'

Then he wondered where that voice was coming from. A shudder went through him as he remembered the devil. He had been taught to avoid him when he was a child, but he had ignored such warning in adult life. Yet he could not help think that the devil might be correct. Would God really forgive Billy Bray?

This new thought troubled him. Was the devil telling the truth? On the other hand, he had heard someone say that God will forgive the vilest sinner if he truly believes in Jesus.[3] Billy turned over the page of his hymn book and read, 'Jesus ready stands

[3] These are lines from the hymn, 'To God be the Glory, great things he has done,' but it was written in 1875, seven years after Billy went to be with the Lord forever.

to save you.'[4] A sudden hope flooded his mind and suddenly he fell on his knees again in an attitude of prayer as he pleaded, 'Will you save even a sinner as bad as me?'

With all these thoughts skimming around in his mind, Billy finally got up from his knees and went downstairs to join Joey. He apologised that he had neglected her all day, but she said, 'Billy, I know that you have a lot of things to sort out.'

Although she was still worried about her husband, Joey had a strange feeling that all would soon be well and their life would change forever.

---

[4] Hymn No. 324 from the hymn that starts, 'Come, ye sinners poor and wretched.'

The Devil Challenged

That Saturday night Billy slept well, but when he awoke next morning he had an uneasy feeling. Instead of jumping off his bed and going out into the garden to do a few jobs, as he usually did on Sunday mornings, he just lay on the bed and looked up at the ceiling. The small cracks in the plaster and the rather large spider crawling across it, did not hold his attention.

He heard Joey moving around downstairs and so he forced himself off the bed and went down the rickety stairs. She had already lit the fire and the smell of porridge cheered him up a little, but he still felt restless. During breakfast, he usually thought about which smutty stories he would tell his friends the following week. Today, all those unhelpful thoughts were far from his mind and he wondered what the future held. Billy stood up and stared out of the window.

'Come on Billy,' said Joey. 'Sit down and eat your meal before it gets cold. Winter's coming on and you need to build up your strength.' Billy realised he had been a thoughtless husband and asked himself, 'How does Joey manage to provide so much food for us and our children, when I give her so little money?' For the first time in his life, he began to realise how wrong he had been to spend his wages on beer and give so little to his wife to buy the needs of the household.

He picked at his food, but left most of it. Then he stood up and announced, 'It's Sunday.' It was the first word he had uttered that day and Joey wondered why he told her what she already knew.

Billy spoke again, 'It's only a mile to the house where those Bible Christians have their class meeting on Sunday mornings. I think I'll go and see what happens there.'

Joey had never known Billy to show any interest in church or chapel before and she wondered what, if anything, she should say. In the silence she suddenly became aware of the beat of the rain as it pelted hard on the cottage roof. 'You'll get soaked if you go out in this weather,' said Joey. 'It's not sensible to go out in this downpour when you have the chance to stay here in the warm, and be dry.' But Billy had made up his mind so she let him go to the door. 'Goodbye love. I'll be waiting for you when you get back,' she called after him as he strode out into the deluge.

As he brushed the wet from his face, Billy tried to remember what happened at class meetings. He knew they were not proper services with a preacher and singers. They were just little house meetings where the leader of the class encouraged them all to speak about some of the things that had happened to them during the previous week.

Billy liked the idea that there was no sermon, but he wondered what he would say if he was asked to share his experiences of the week. Would they laugh at him if he told about his fear of hell?

He had not decided what to say by the time he saw the house in front of him. Marching up to the door of the house he banged on the door knocker. Eventually he found himself gazing into the anxious face of an elderly lady. 'I've come to the class meeting,' he spluttered out.

Surprise showed on her face because she recognised him. 'I'm sorry Billy, but no one has come this morning because the weather is too bad for them.'

Billy, frustrated, turned around and set off for home again. His thoughts about the Bible Christians were not complimentary. 'If they allow a little rain to keep them from God's house then they won't be able to do me any good,' he grumbled.

'That was a very short meeting,' said Joey as Billy opened the door on his return home. 'Yes,' said her husband, 'and it will be a long time before I seek their help again.'

She stood back and waited for him to vent his anger, but instead he moved gently towards her, placed his arms round her shoulders and sobbed deeply. 'I'll never find peace, Joey, and I'm so ashamed of the way I've treated you with all my drinking and foul language.'

Joey began to weep also.

'We've both ignored God and not followed the teaching of the Lord.' Then Joey screamed out in sorrow, 'What is going to become of us and the children? We are all so sinful.'

Eventually they both stopped crying and sat down in front of the fire. Billy dried off his wet clothes, but his heart was still heavy with the weight of his sin. 'I must find peace,' said Billy. 'I must find peace with God, even if I can't find happiness.'

With that he picked up his Bible and his hymn book and slunk off to the bedroom again. All afternoon he cried out to the Lord for mercy and the whole time the devil tempted him and told him that it was all a delusion. 'You'll never find mercy,' he sneered.

All of these thoughts bombarded Billy's troubled mind. Then some words came to him. He picked up his Bible and started searching for the half-remembered word. Eventually he found it in the Sermon on the Mount, 'Ask, and it will be given to you; seek and you shall find; knock and the door will be opened to you' (Matthew 7:7).

Reading those words gave him some comfort, but they also reminded him of his grandfather. What were the words that grandfather loved to say? Then he found the place, "For I know the plans I have for you," declares the Lord, "plans to prosper you and not to harm you, plans to give you hope and a future. Then you will call upon me and come and pray to me, and I will listen to you. You will seek me and find me when you seek me with all your heart" (Jeremiah 29:11-13).'

'Listen to that, devil,' shouted Billy. 'God says that he doesn't think evil thoughts about me and he tells me that if I seek him with all my heart I will find him. That is exactly what I am going to do, so stop telling me that I'll never find him.'

Joey was relieved when she saw Billy's face as he came back downstairs for his supper. 'What was all that shouting?' said Joey.

'Oh that,' said Billy. 'I was just telling the devil that he was wrong and that if we sought the Lord with all our hearts then we would find him.'

A much calmer atmosphere then flooded over them and they were more contented as they ate their food and then went up to bed.

Billy still had not found the happiness he sought, but he had learned to ignore the devil's lies.

The following morning Billy got out of bed and went on his knees once more in order to resume his quest for mercy. It was then that he saw the second verse of the hymn he had been reading. Could this really be true?

[Jesus] now stands knocking at the door
Of every sinner's heart?

'Not mine', thought Billy. 'He won't want my wicked heart.' But the hymn continued,

The worst need keep him out no more,
Or force him to depart.[1]

---

[1] Hymn No. 333 in the Methodist Hymn Book, 1933 edition.

Billy wondered how Mr Wesley knew what he was thinking, particularly as it had been one hundred years since he wrote that verse. Billy looked at the words again. 'The worst need keep him out no more.' Then he said to himself, 'I must be the worst sinner in Cornwall so is Mr Wesley telling me that I need not keep the Lord out of my life any longer?'

Billy stood up. He did not know whether to be relieved or discouraged, but he believed that the Lord Jesus Christ wanted to come into his life. He started to wonder whether it was his pride that was keeping the Lord out.

Billy reluctantly closed his Bible and his hymn book and got himself ready for his afternoon shift down the mine.

The Devil Defeated

Billy wasn't his usual jokey self as he made his way down the pit. His work-mates noticed the change.

He pretended not to notice when one of the men muttered, 'What's wrong with Billy today? He's usually full of wise-cracks.' In the past, Billy would leap to his defence if he heard anyone criticising him. Today he said nothing.

As he worked, he soon found a rhythm as he swung his hammer at the rock-face. Each time it smashed down he cried out in his mind, 'Lord, have mer-cy-on-me. Lord, have mer-cy-on-me.' Although he spoke no words out loud, his mind was working overtime. The whole afternoon he pleaded with God to forgive him.

On his long walk home each step he took echoed with this question, 'Will I ever find peace?'

The following day Billy only spoke to his work-mates if they asked him a question. At the end of the shift he returned home in the same state as he had done the day before.

The next morning, after breakfast, Billy again took his Bible and his hymn book and went up to the bedroom. Again and again he prayed, 'Lord, have mercy on me.' He opened his hymn book and read some more of Mr Wesley's words. It seemed to him as if peace had come nearer. As he looked up, his eye caught a movement outside. It was a sparrow flying freely. 'If only I could be as free as that bird,' he thought. 'That creature has no burden of sin to carry, as I have.' He was about to burst into tears once again when his eyes read these words,

> When shall thy love constrain,
> And force me to thy breast?
> When shall my soul return again?
> To her eternal rest?[1]

'Yes, Lord, that's what I need. I want your love to force me to come to you and find you.' As he thought about those words it seemed as though God was reaching down, taking him in his arms and lifting him towards heaven.

'If only I had just a little more faith,' thought Billy. 'Then I'd receive God's mercy.'

While he was trying to compose his thoughts, Joey called up the stairs, 'It's time, Billy.'

On his walk to the mine, the same thoughts kept going round his head. The only thing he needed in the whole wide world was to be assured that the Lord was going to be merciful to him and forgive his sin.

Today Billy had the wheel barrow. His task was to load up the rock and then wheel it to the base of the

---

[1] Hymn 341 in the Methodist Hymnbook, 1933 edition.

ladder and tip it on to the pile of ore that was waiting to be hauled to the surface.

Down below, as he pushed the next load of rock to the loading area, the devil kept tormenting him. But Billy could stand his taunts no longer. He was so angry that he shouted, 'You are a liar, devil.' As soon as he said that it seemed as if the great weight of his sin fell to the ground and rolled away out of his sight.

Billy could scarcely believe what had happened in those split seconds. He finally felt free and 'silent Billy' transformed into a very noisy Billy as he shouted out, 'Glory be to God. Glory be to God.' He danced up and down and roared out, 'I've found mercy at last.'

It was true. The Lord had taken away Billy's guilt and he was no longer sad.

He was so excited, and relieved, that he called to his three companions. 'Come here friends. I've great news for you.' They came running, wondering what ever had happened. They were surprised when Billy said, 'I've found peace with God and I now know what true happiness is. I would rather be hauled to the surface and set on fire with these rocks than go back to my sinful ways again.'

Joey could not believe it when Billy opened the door that night and stood there with a broad smile lighting up his face. 'Something's happened to you,' she blurted out. Billy's grin grew brighter still as he said, 'Yes. I think I'm near the Saviour.' Joey was not quite sure how to reply, but with a cautious voice she muttered, 'How wonderful – now come and sit down and eat your supper and tell me all about it.'

Billy smiled at her pleasantly. He had no wish to upset her so he chose his words very carefully. 'Joey, your suppers are always very delicious, but I want something even better than your food this evening; I want to be alone with the Lord.' He kissed her, picked up his Bible and hymn book and then climbed the stairs. Joey wondered what had caused this change in him, but she was not upset by his refusal of her supper.

She continued quietly with her sewing, but hesitated when she heard him talking in the bedroom. There were no telephones in those days, but Billy was certainly speaking to someone. Then she realised what was happening when he called out, 'Lord, you've said, "Ask and it will be given to you; seek and you will find; knock and the door will be opened to you. For everyone who asks receives; he who seeks finds; and to him who knocks, the door will be opened."[2] Well, I'm asking you now.'

Joey thought back to her young days and she remembered the chapel where she often heard words like those Billy was praying. She listened more intently and heard Billy say, 'Lord, you know that I've been asking, and I've been seeking and I've been knocking at your door. I've been doing just what my neighbour did the other day when he needed my help urgently. You know that I opened my door and invited him into

---

[2] Luke 11:9-10

my house. So, please won't you open the door of your house and let me in?'

Then something happened. Billy's voice bellowed out, 'Glory. Praise be to God for his great salvation.'

A wonderful sense of peace had flooded into Billy's soul as he knelt in the bedroom. He no longer pleaded with God; instead he started shouting with glee, 'Lord, you have saved me, even me, and made me the happiest person in the whole world.'

At that very moment he had a vision of all his sins being borne away by the Lord. He was like a new man waking up in a new world. Billy rushed downstairs and grabbed Joey in his arms. In an excited voice he said, 'I'm a new creation for I've found the Lord. I feel just like Isaiah when he said, "I will praise you, O Lord. Although you were angry with me, your anger has turned away and you have comforted me."[3] That's how it is with me now dear; everything is new.'

Billy's new birth reminded Joey of the time when she first asked Jesus into her life. Seeing what a change had come over her husband she again longed to know the joy of God's salvation.

When Billy set Joey down, a sense of quietness came over him and then a look of sadness as he told her how sorry he was for his behaviour when he was drunk. He sat her on his knee and said, 'These past days my mind has been in turmoil because I could not

---

[3] Isaiah 12:1

believe the Lord would ever forgive me. But, praise his name, he has forgiven me.'

He tried to explain his feelings. 'Do you remember that David sinned with Bathsheba?'

Yes, Joey certainly remembered that story, and what a sad one it was.

Then Billy smiled and told her, 'If God could forgive David, who was such an important man then surely he can forgive me because I'm of no value in this world.' Then he opened his Bible and said, 'Listen to this dear, David wrote, "I waited patiently for the Lord; he turned to me and heard my cry. He lifted me out of the slimy pit, out of the mud and mire; he set my feet on a rock and gave me a firm place to stand. He put a new song in my mouth, a hymn of praise to our God".[4] Well, Joey, he's done the same for me, praise his wonderful name.'

They spent a long time talking about how their lives were going to be different from that moment onwards. In a soft and sweet voice he told her, 'Life is going to be better, much, much better my darling. I want to tell everyone about my Lord.'

Joey had no wish to dampen her husband's enthusiasm so she said nothing for a while but eventually she whispered, 'Billy, do you realise that the men at the mine will find it difficult to believe that you are a changed man? They'll try to win you back on to their side.'

---

[4] Psalm 40:1-3

Billy looked very serious and then said, 'I know they will, particularly as I've been their 'chairman' for so many years. They'll be expecting me to tell them dirty stories, but I will show them that I have now finished with all that filth and those lies. God has said in his word, "I am making everything new,"[5] and that means me too. I am a new creation because the Lord Jesus is living in me now and so my life is going to be different.'

Joey began to relax. She loved her husband even more because she could sense that what had happened to him was real. If he was determined to live as a Christian, then she was certain he would never go back to his old ways.

As they made their way up to bed, Billy exclaimed out loud, 'Jesus is now my own Saviour and my friend. I'm ashamed to say that I used to be a servant of the devil, but from now onwards I'm going to be a servant of the Lord.'

---

[5] Revelation 21:5

Friends or Enemies?

The next morning, the frost glistened as the rays of the sun hit the top of the garden pump. Joey looked out the window and saw something very unusual; the top of the pump was frosty, but its handle was clear. She turned back to the fire with a puzzled expression on her face. As she put another log on it she saw a bucket of water standing on the hearth. Then she understood. Her Billy had been up earlier and pumped up the water from their well. 'He's a good man,' she said to herself. Like all the other men, Billy thought that getting the water from the well was women's work. But today he had done that instead of his wife.

Seeing the frost outside, reminded her that the severest winter days would soon be upon them. Shivering, she pulled her old coat more closely around her.

As Joey set out the breakfast, she thought about all the different ways she had used to try to make their small amount of food look more appetising. Life was hard for her and her neighbours, but she was not sad. She felt the cold air on her hands, yet a warm glow spread from inside of her. For most of her married life she had worried about her Billy, particularly as he wasted so much money on drink, but now he was a different man. What were the words he had used to describe himself? 'I'm a new man, Joey. I'm a changed man.'

The fire that Billy had lit earlier was now burning brightly. Then she heard the click of the door latch and, looking up, saw her new man entering the room from the garden. Billy's face broke into a broad smile when he saw the breakfast on the table. He suddenly rushed towards her, threw his strong arms around her and lifted her into the air. A warm thrill ran through her body as Billy put her down again and kissed her on her cheek with great tenderness. 'Today is going to be the start of a new life for us all,' he announced, still grinning broadly. 'I now see why my granddad was always so bright and cheerful. It was because he knew the same joy of the Lord that I feel today.'

As they sat and ate their breakfast, Joey became troubled about the reaction of the other men at the mine. She knew that they would be very cross when they learned that Billy had 'gone all religious', and they would want to win him back to their side. She shared her concerns with Billy who understood her anxiety, but he could not stay away from his old friends. 'I have a command from God to go and tell everyone that Jesus has died to take away sin,' Billy explained. 'If I avoid them now, they're going to say, "He thinks that he's too good for the likes of us."'

Billy knew that the men would take his conversion as a challenge to win him back to the side of the devil. But Billy got up from the table, put on his coat and kissed his wife, and the children, and left.

That day Joey found it difficult to concentrate on her housework. It was comforting to know that her man had found the Lord. 'But what about me?' she thought. 'Will I ever become a true Christian again?'

Frowning, Joey wondered, 'Why did I stop going to chapel?' She knew that Billy was not the cause, because she had drifted away long before she fell in love with him. She still believed, in a kind of way, but she did not have the joy in Jesus that her husband had now found.

As Joey busied herself with the house and her children, the time sped by. The baby took a lot of extra time. Soon it became dark and she knew that her man, her new man, would be home before long.

She soon heard his footsteps approaching the house. She could tell it was him because he always walked with a jumping movement. In any case, she had heard his singing before he came into sight. Finally, he was in her welcoming arms.

Joey's questions tumbled out so quickly that Billy started laughing. 'Hold hard my dear,' he said. 'Give me a moment and I'll tell you all about it.'

Billy then sat down beside his wife and began to tell her the story of his day. 'I told them. I told them that I was now happy in the Lord. And do you know some of them looked really sad. One said, "You're mad, but we'll get you back next pay-day. Once you've got some ale inside of you, you'll forget all about praising the Lord and that kind of stuff."'

'Do you know, Joey, I kept calm. I really did. I don't know how I achieved it because if they had spoken to me like that before I found the Lord, I would have flown into a rage. I just looked at them and said, "You think I'm a mad man. I'll tell you what I am, I'm a glad man and I just want to praise the Lord and tell you what you're missing."'

Billy continued with the story of the day's events, 'Then they said they were upset because I used to entertain them with dirty stories that made them laugh. I just told them that I had a new story to tell now, about heaven and heavenly things. They won't just make you laugh; they'll make you happy and give you joy that goes deep down into your souls.'

Witnessing for Christ

Although the weather was growing colder, Billy was filled with a warm sense of joy and he took that happiness with him everywhere he went. It had always been his nature to make people laugh. Before he was saved he did it to make people like him, but now he wanted to make people happy for the glory of God. He could not understand why those who went to church and chapel kept quiet about their faith in Jesus. He did exactly the opposite. He had always been a great chatterer, but now Jesus was the subject of almost every conversation. His faith in Christ flowed out from him like a swollen stream after heavy rain.

The change in him was obvious to everyone. Some of his workmates now started to make fun of him, but their sneering soon ceased. Although they did not understand how Billy could have altered so radically, they could not fail to like him.

Billy talked to people about his Lord. When he was on his own he loved to read his Bible. The late November evenings were getting darker and so he and Joey spent them around the fireside. He loved to talk to her about some of the things he was learning about Jesus. Joey taught Billy some of the songs from her childhood in chapel and Billy found others in the hymn book. He especially loved those that had helped him so much when he was seeking the Lord.

On every suitable occasion, Billy shared his Christian faith with his fellow miners. One day he overheard one of them say, 'He won't be able to keep that up. You mark my words, as soon as he hits trouble he'll be back supping the ale again.'

Billy said nothing. He just smiled to himself. Only a few weeks previously he would have been irritated with such words, but now the deep peace of Christ gave him a calmness he had never known before.

He was surprised at the attitude of those miners who professed to be Christians. He had seen them on their way to the Methodist chapel each Sunday, walking along wearing their respectable clothes and Sunday hats, but he had never seen any of them praying. He asked himself, 'Why didn't they tell me that I would end up in hell if I didn't repent and turn to Christ? Why are they so secretive and unloving when I want to share everything I know about Jesus with other people?'

One day when he was working with his friend, Joseph, he asked him, 'Did those people, who went to church and chapel ever tell you about the Lord Jesus Christ and how he died to save us from our sins?'

Joseph looked surprised at the question and then turned away. 'No,' he muttered. 'They keep themselves to themselves and don't worry us with their religious talk.'

The next time they had a break, Billy asked, 'Joseph, those men we were talking about earlier, did they never pray with you when you were on the same work-party as them?'

'No,' said his friend, 'I told you. They never bothered us with that kind of stuff and that's the way I like it,' he snapped.

One day Billy decided to do something quite different at work.

It was the habit of every gang of workers to stand in a group near the foot of the ladder at the start of each shift. They waited there for the team leader to organise their work. Billy was now a team leader, but instead of giving them orders he said, 'Friends, I want to pray for our work-party today. It's very dangerous down here and we need the Lord's protection.'

This surprised the men; they had never started with prayer. He surprised them even more when he said, 'I'm going to pray that if any of us are killed this day, that it will be me.'

'Hang on Billy,' said one of his gang, 'why you?' Billy looked at him and smiled and said, 'If any of you die you will go straight to hell because you don't know the Lord as your Saviour, and I don't want you to be lost. But if I have to die today, then I know that I'll be with God before you even start to climb up those ladders and go home for your tea.'

As he finished his prayer with a loud, 'Amen', Billy immediately stooped to pick up his things and started to walk to his allotted place. He glanced up as he left the others and noticed that several of them had tears in their eyes. He made a mental note of their names and decided to pray for each of them. He longed that they would be as happy in the Lord as he was.

Billy was paired with his good friend Justin Thomas from Devonshire days. As soon as they reached the place they were to work at, they set to. They knew they would only be paid for the amount of tin their rocks contained. They first of all attacked the rocks with their hammers and picks, then they stopped and broke the fallen pieces of rock into easily-managed sizes. Because the work was very hard, they had a short break every now and then so they could get their breaths back. During one of these pauses, Billy said, 'Justin, do you remember how we loved to get drunk when we were in Devonshire? I used to think it was great fun to wake up in a muddy bog by the side of the track because we were so befuddled by the drink. I realise now how foolish that was.'

Justin looked at him with a pained expression. 'Billy, you only think it was foolish because you're a man now and you need the money to support your wife and family.'

'No,' said Billy. 'I'm saying this because now I know the Lord. I understand how wicked it was to behave like that. It was wicked, because we were disobeying God's laws. I'm a new person now and I'm heading for heaven, but I'm concerned about you. If you die without knowing the Lord as your Saviour, then you'll go to hell and suffer for your sins. And that pain will go on forever.'

Justin looked shocked. Before Billy could say another word his companion turned away, picked up his shovel and mumbled, 'Come on Billy. We must get more of this stuff to the surface otherwise we won't earn very much. Let's get moving again.'

They said very little during the rest of their shift until it was time to meet up with the others at the foot of the ladders. As they waited for all of the gang to join them someone from back in the tunnel whispered, 'Billy's a fool. I liked him much better before he caught religion.'

Immediately, Justin turned upon the man and spoke sharply to him. There was too much chattering going on around him for Billy to catch what he said, but, as they were climbing the ladders, one of the others said to Billy, 'Did you notice that one of the lads called you a fool? Justin told him to leave you alone. I was standing right next to him and he said he knew you before you had changed.'

Billy thought for a while and then said, 'I'm glad he spoke up for me.' As they continued climbing the other man said, 'Justin told me that he wished he was like you and enjoyed the peace of God.'

Billy said nothing because a sudden surge of love for Justin flooded his soul. As he placed each foot on the next rung of the ladder, he prayed, 'Lord, please save dear Justin.' This was his prayer, over and over again until he reached the surface of the ground.

Billy had begun to write down a prayer list. On it he wrote the names of everyone he was praying for. When he got home, he added Justin to it. His prayer-time was no chore. He had plenty to talk to the Lord about as he told his dear Lord about everything he had done that day.

A few days later, when the weather had become a little milder, Billy was busy out in his garden. Just then he had a sudden overwhelming urge to pray for Justin. Although the ground was muddy, Billy dropped on to his knees and prayed, 'O Lord, do save my friend, Justin. You saved someone as sinful as I was, so please save dear Justin?'

But as he prayed about Justin, he felt strange. It was as though the Lord was telling him, 'I will save Justin very soon.' Billy knew that this was a message from God. In the coming days and years, Billy was often going to 'hear' God's voice like that and he seldom had doubts about what God meant.

As Billy was meditating about these things, Joey called to him from the kitchen. 'It's time for you to come in and get ready for your afternoon shift, Billy.' He got up from his knees, washed himself at the kitchen sink and got ready for work. Since he found the Lord, he never left the house without praying with Joey. After he had done so he kissed her an affectionate 'goodbye' and set out for work.

He arrived at the mine in plenty of time. As he started his descent down the ladders he heard the morning shift climbing upward. Peering down, he saw the hand of the first miner reaching upward. It carried a pick and he recognised it as that of his friend, Justin. In that instant, Billy knew that God wanted him to speak to Justin, to tell him what he had told Billy that afternoon.

When Justin got on a level with him, Billy smiled and said, 'I've got some good news for you. While I was out in the field praying for you, the Lord told me you will be converted very soon.'

Justin did not know quite what to say, so he just murmured, 'thank you' and carried on his way up to the surface.

Shortly after that, Justin came to know the Lord Jesus as his Saviour. However, before many months had passed, he became sick and soon had to take to his bed. Billy visited him many times and Justin died happy in the Lord.

After his funeral, Billy gladly told Justin's work-mates, 'Brother Justin is now with Abraham and Isaac and Jacob in the kingdom of heaven, praising God and he will praise him for ever and ever.

Chapel Life

'Joey, do you realise this is my first Sunday as a man who is happy in the Lord?' Billy smiled as he gathered his wife up in his arms and whispered, 'Although I've always been very happy with you, Joey, I'm even more excited now I know the Lord as my Saviour.'

Billy gazed out of the tiny window in their bedroom and saw a gloomy November day. The air was damp with fog and normally that weather would make him feel depressed. Today was different. His heart leaped with joy as he looked at his small garden with new eyes. The gloom of the day was suddenly lifted as a sudden shaft of sunlight shot across the countryside and lit everything up.

He turned to his wife and said, 'Can you see the sun peeping up over the hill and shining through the mist, Joey? I have a feeling that the Lord Jesus is going to light up the whole village. All these years I've been living in the gloom of sin, but now the Sun of Righteousness has risen with healing in his wings[1]. You know what the good book says, "This is the day the Lord has made; let us rejoice and be glad in it."'[2]

[1] See Malachi 4:2
[2] Psalm 118:24

Joey giggled and felt very contented. What a change had come over her Billy. Usually he stayed in bed on Sunday morning to sleep off the effects of all the beer he had drunk the night before. Today, her Billy was a new person.

His smile lit up his face as he said, 'I'm going to chapel this morning. Hicks Mill Chapel is only a few miles from here and it will make a nice walk.'

Joey looked anxiously at her husband's tatty trousers and patched jacket. 'Do you think it will be all right for you to go to chapel wearing those clothes? Everyone puts on their Sunday best to go to chapel?'

There was a slightly anxious look on Billy's face, but it quickly disappeared as he said, 'The Bible tells us that 'man looks at the outward appearance but God looks at the heart.[3]' I'm sure they will accept me as I am, just as the Lord has.'

Billy knew that the people who went to the Methodist Chapel were very particular about the way they dressed. They were more formal than the Christian meeting place that Billy had gone to the other week.

He looked down at his trousers and jacket. Perhaps for the first time in his life he became aware that they were shabby, but he turned to Joey and said, 'They're clean aren't they? You make sure of that because you're a good wife.' He picked up his old, tatty hat and kissed Joey 'goodbye.' As he closed the door behind him he

---

[3] See 1 Samuel 16:7

said, 'My coat may be shabby, but my heart has been washed clean in the precious blood of Christ.'

As he climbed the rough road that ran up from the village, he wondered what he would find at the Hicks Mill Chapel. He carried his Bible and was proud that he could read it. He was pleased too, that he could quote much of it by heart. He started to sing as he walked along. Instead of singing naughty words as he was used to doing, he sang of the Lord and his goodness.

Eventually, he came into the village and could see the simple little chapel. He took a deep breath and opened the door. There were already quite a few people in their seats; most of them were chattering to their neighbours. As he moved forward, the hum of conversation died away and he realised that people were looking at him.

Billy's reputation for being fearless was well known in that area, but he now felt over-awed in the presence of these people as they gathered to worship his new Master, the Lord Jesus. Since he had been made happy in the Lord, his attitude to others had changed. Before his conversion, Joey and the children had been the most important people in his life. Now he felt differently; he had no wish to give offence to anyone. Thinking of this made him wonder where he could sit. He remembered that some people paid rents for special seats, so he had no wish to sit in one of those. 'Surely there are some spare seats at the back where anyone could sit,' he thought. A movement at the front of the chapel made him realise that the meeting was about to commence, so he quickly slid into an empty seat near the door.

Immediately in front of the reading desk, some of the pews had been put into an oblong shape. He then heard a low note sound and saw a man begin to tune up a cello. Next to him was another man who held a wooden flute up to his lips; and a third person placed a small violin under his chin.

Another man who was dressed in dark clothes got up from his seat and moved to the preacher's chair. Then a deacon, who had been sitting at the desk in front of the pulpit, stood up. He cleared his throat and said, 'Friends, we will sing hymn number 346,

> O Jesus, full of truth and grace,
> More full of grace than I of sin,
> Yet once again I seek Thy face;
> Open Thine arms, and take me in,
> And freely my backslidings heal,
> And love the faithless sinner still.'

Everyone rose from their seats. The musicians played over the tune and everyone sang that verse. As Billy sang, his eyes filled with tears at the knowledge that God's grace was bigger and more powerful even than his own sin. He almost broke down at the wonder of those words and could scarce hold back the sobs while the deacon read the words of the next verse before they all sang:

Thou know'st the way to bring me back,
My fallen spirit to restore;
O for Thy truth and mercy's sake,
Forgive, and bid me sin no more;
The ruins of my soul repair,
And make my heart a house of prayer.

The deacon continued to read out each verse before the people sang it. For a moment, Billy was proud of himself because he could read and did not need anyone to tell him the words of the next verse. He immediately became convicted of his sin. 'What have I got to be proud of, just because I can read? These unlearned folk around me are much better people than I, because I have sinned so grievously.' He smiled to himself and thought, 'The Lord, though, is more full of truth and grace than I am of sin.'

When the preacher thanked God for taking away his sin, Billy uttered 'Amen and Amen'. He kept saying this all through the simple prayer.

He was still thinking of that prayer when the preacher read from the Bible and they sang their next hymn. He listened to the sermon intently and wanted to shout out 'Hallelujah, praise the Lord' several times as the preacher emphasised the wonderful truths of the gospel.

Not many people called out things at his grandfather's chapel, but the congregation at Hicks Mill Chapel called out praises to God, time and time again. Before long Billy joined with them in his praise to the Lord for his goodness and grace.

After the service was over, Billy politely bowed his head like all the others. He sat there for a moment and then the preacher moved over to where he was sitting and said, 'It's nice to see you here friend.' Some of the other people chatted to him as well. Billy told them about how he had recently become happy in the Lord and how his life was now going to be lived for the glory of God.

As he headed for home, he had a merry feeling in his soul. Even the strength of the chill wind did not dampen his spirits. He arrived home in no time and called out, 'Joey. I've had a wonderful time with those people and I think we should make Hicks Mill our own chapel.'

Joey gave her husband a sad smile. 'I'm so pleased you are happy Billy, but I'm afraid I'm still far off from God. However hard I try, I just can't find the joy that you know.'

'Come here my lovely wife,' said Billy as he picked her up in his arms. 'Soon you will also be brought into God's family. I know it deep down in my soul.'

Billy, the Dancer and Singer

A few days after Billy's conversion his team were working at the mine head. Their task that day was to move some of the larger pieces of rock which had been brought up from below. As they were doing this, Billy noticed someone staring at him. After a while the man said, 'Why are you happy, Billy? You don't earn any more money than the rest of us and your home is no better than ours, but whatever you're doing, you can't seem to stop singing.'

Billy looked closely at the man and smiled. 'I'm happy because the Lord has saved me and promised me a home in heaven when I die.' Immediately, he started to jump up and down and sing at the top of his voice. His colleague leaned on his shovel and stared. Then the Captain, the only man in the mine who didn't like Billy, shouted, 'Stop that silliness, Mr Bray.' Then in a softer tone the Captain turned to Billy and said, 'You wouldn't leap and dance and make all that fuss if you were in an unsteady tunnel deep underground, would you? So why do you do it here in the open air?'

Although the rest of the men kept working, they all stole a glance in Billy's direction and wondered how he would react to the Captain's rebuke. All that

Billy said was, 'My Captain, I dance and sing because I am contented in my work. The Lord is my great big Captain in the sky and he has made me happy.' The Captain stared at him for a moment and then turned away mumbling, 'Get on with your work, all of you.'

From that moment on the Captain took a dislike to Mr Bray, as he called him.

Every Sunday morning, the Captain went to a 'respectable' chapel where everything was done in an orderly manner. He had no liking for all the 'calling out' and 'praising the Lord' that he heard went on at Hicks Mill Chapel. He believed that what he called frivolous behaviour should be avoided in chapel. He decided to watch Billy very closely and planned to get his own back.

It was not long after that incident, that the Captain was again around when Billy's shift was on duty. He called Billy over to him. 'Mr Bray, I am coming to work alongside you and your mate today. We'll go down the mine together and I'll make sure you work so hard that you won't have time to do all that leaping and jumping and praising the Lord nonsense.'

Billy had always been a good worker, and so was his Captain. That morning they all hacked out a great deal of ore from one of the most difficult places in the mine. Every time Billy stopped for breath, the Captain scowled at him and nodded his head to urge him to get back to his work. The Captain was waiting for the opportunity to mock Billy and tell him what he thought of as his 'unnecessary' religious fervour.

Every now and then the men stopped for a short breather. Each time they just let their tools fall to the ground, because they were so tired. However, because the Captain was with them, they placed them down very carefully. They were working at the far end of a tunnel and soon noticed water seeping in from the sea. It gathered on the floor in an increasingly large puddle. It was not unusual for water to come into the tunnel, but care had to be taken because it was often contaminated with poisonous salts. They certainly had to make sure that none of it splashed into their eyes.

At every break, the Captain took the opportunity to mock Billy. Billy thought, 'I mustn't get angry, but I'm not sure how much more I can take of this.' Yet he knew that the Lord was with him, and that day he felt an extra sense of God's presence. Later he was to realise it was the Holy Spirit, God's power, at work in his life.

He suddenly stopped worrying about becoming angry. It was as though the Lord had grabbed him under his arms and lifted him up. Immediately, he began to jump up and shout 'praise the Lord'. He did so with such enthusiasm, that the water started to splash up into his face. As he bounded higher still the water splashed up and extinguished his candle. Strangely, his eyes did not sting from the water and he cared little about his candle because he felt that the light of God was shining into his heart.

However, some of the water splashed his Captain. Billy failed to notice this in his joy. But the Captain was not cross. Instead he shook his head, as he had done before. He turned to Billy's fellow-worker and asked, 'Is this a mad man that you have working with you?'

Later, when Billy got home from work, he told Joey about his experience of the Lord's presence in the mine. 'It was wonderful Joey. I wish you could know more of God's power. The Captain said that I was a mad man, but I'm not. I'm a glad man and the Lord has made me one. David was not mad when he danced before the Lord, even though his wife thought he was behaving shamefully.'[1]

Joey did not know what to say. She loved her husband but she wondered if he had gone too far this time. As gently as she could, she whispered, 'I do wish you would be careful dear. I don't want you upsetting the Captain because we depend on him and the work he gives you to do. Do you realise that if you have no work we will all starve to death?'

Billy took Joey in his arms and placed a soft kiss on her sweet mouth. 'My darling, darling Joey, you know you mean everything to me – you and the little ones the Lord has given us – but the Lord Jesus Christ has an even greater place in my life. It is he who has made me so happy. That's why I want to dance and leap for joy, because of his goodness to us all. David's Lord is

[1] See 2 Samuel 6:21-22

my Lord; bless his holy name. If a man will not leap and dance for heaven, what will he leap and dance for? There is no better prize than heaven.'

He then told her about a story he had been reading in the Bible the previous day. It was about Abraham going to sacrifice his only son, because God told him to do so. What a blessing it was that he was stopped at the last moment. He smiled at his wife and said, 'Do you know what Abraham called that place, Joey? He called it, "The Lord will provide."[2] St Paul wrote to the church at Philippi and told them, "My God will meet all your needs."[3] Listen to me Joey; that same Lord will surely provide for the needs of each one of us.'

Joey smiled at her loved one and then let him continue to tell her about the events of the day.

'Do you know what that Captain said? He told me that Christians should not leap and dance and shout so much. I said that the Lord knows everyone's heart and then I said, "And he knows your heart too." Do you know what he said to me then Joey? He said, "Now look here, Mr holy-man Bray, the Lord isn't deaf so we don't need to shout at him."'

'I hope you didn't say anything more Billy,' said Joey, with a pleading tone.

'Oh yes I did,' said Billy. 'I told him, "The devil isn't deaf either, but why do the devil's servants make such a great noise?" I told him that people like him

<hr>

[2] Genesis 22:14
[3] Philippians 4:19

were like the devil. I said, "The devil doesn't want to hear us shouting; he wants to see us doubting." The Captain didn't know how to answer that one, and just turned away and went back into his office.'

'Do you know, Joey, we Christians have a right to shout, and must because we have a great deal to shout about? Those Christian people who don't know the joy of the Lord see no need to shout. Sometimes I wonder whether they really know the Lord at all.'

Billy went on to explain that the formal Christians were just like the Pharisees of Jesus' day. 'They dress in their nice Sunday best clothes and go to chapel but I wonder whether they have ever repented of their sin and found the Lord as their Saviour.'

Billy was in full flow now and said, 'When the Lord and his disciples approached Jerusalem and the people spread their coats on the ground to make the road easier for the donkey to walk on, all the people shouted out. They cried, "Blessed is the king who comes in the name of the Lord."'

'Now, Joey, do you remember what the Pharisees said about that? They said to Jesus, "Teacher, rebuke your disciples." But the Lord turned to them and said, "If they keep quiet, the stones will cry out."[4] Joey, I think those so-called Christians who think we are wrong to be joyful in the Lord are no better than those Pharisees of the Lord's day.'

[4] See Luke 19:39-40

Billy's First Chapel Testimony

Hicks Mill Chapel became Billy's spiritual home from the very first Sunday of his new life of happiness. Even though he had worked very hard from Monday to Saturday each week, Billy refused to stay in bed on Sundays. After breakfast it became his habit to walk to his new chapel. He no longer worried whether his clothes were smart enough, because he knew he was not the only man who had no 'Sunday best' clothes to wear.

After a few weeks Joey said, 'Billy, can I come with you next Sunday morning?' It had been a very long time since she had been to chapel. She was a little nervous, but had seen such a change in Billy's life that she could no longer stay at home while he went to Hicks Mill.

On the Saturday morning, she washed the children's things ready for chapel, but was a little sad because she had no fancy clothes for them to wear. However, the coarse material from which she had made their clothes was strong. It would last far longer than the fine silks worn by the rich people. The next Sunday was a bright winter day and the whole family set out. 'At least we are all clean, even if we are dressed very plainly,' thought Joey.

As they opened the chapel door, the class meeting was about to begin. Class leaders were members of the congregation. Their task was to encourage church members to share their Christian experience with the rest of the people gathered for worship.

So far, Billy had kept quiet at these meetings, but on that particular day, in front of his wife and children, he stood up to speak. In very simple words he told them all that his life had been a disappointment to his godly grandfather. He spoke about his drunkenness and how he had turned his back upon chapel-going. 'Then four months ago, the Lord convicted me of my sin. I knew that if I died, as several of my friends have done, I would go straight to hell.'

As he got further into his subject, Billy became more excited and his words flowed freely. He became more animated as he spoke about the joy that he now had. He knew for certain that his sins had been taken away and he was bound for heaven. While he was telling the people how he was now trying to live his life for God, he heard someone sobbing, very quietly. He paused and turned to see where the sound was coming from. The sobbing grew louder and then he saw it was his dear Joey who was weeping uncontrollably. As he stopped talking and bent down to try to comfort her, he heard her whisper, 'Lord, I've been a great sinner and I've turned away from your paths. Please, please forgive me and save me.'

Then Joey stood up. Her eyes were glistening with tears, but there was something else there as well. She grew quiet again and said, 'Thank you Lord. Thank you. Thank you for saving me and bringing me back into your house.' By now her face was shining and not just because it was wet with tears. It glistened with the light of God's Spirit who was flowing in her life.

It was now Billy's turn to sob and through his tears he turned again to the people around him. 'Look, friends. See how gracious the Lord is. First I came to the Lord and now my dear Joey has returned and found the joy of Christ's salvation. What joy there is among the angels in heaven this morning.'

After gathering his wife and children in his arms, Billy started to dance up and down between rows of pews. Over and over again he shouted, 'Glory, glory, hallelujah, praise the Lord.'

Immediately shouts of 'Praise the Lord' and 'Bless his holy name' could be heard coming from every part of the chapel. It went on for a very long time as different people started to call out to God in a prayer of thanksgiving and praise. The joy of the people was so immense, that even the most timid souls began to call out in praise to the Lord Almighty.

That was the first time that Billy spoke in chapel. For the next forty years his voice would not just boom around Hicks Mill Chapel; many churches, chapels and meeting halls in Cornwall and Devonshire would quiver with that cracked, almost tuneless voice. It would ring out, 'Glory, glory, glory; Hallelujah, praise the Lord.'

Billy's First Sermon

By now the whole of Billy's life was surrounded by prayer. His prayers were simple. He just talked to the Lord about whatever was on his mind.

Billy prayed anywhere and everywhere. He shared his thoughts with his Lord as he clambered down the steep grassy banks and climbed up the other side again. He did not make decisions first and then ask God to bless them. He continually asked God for guidance in his work and in his family life. Since he had become 'happy in the Lord' (as he put it) his life was new, fresh and vibrant; prayer came to him as naturally as breathing.

Billy always had a sharp, twinkling eye that beamed out from under his black bushy eyebrows. It was said that every time Billy entered a darkened woodland, it would be lit up immediately by his smile. He had always chattered to friends or strangers that he met on his walks. Now he was a real Christian, he asked them questions like; 'How is your soul today?' or 'Are you rejoicing in the Lord's goodness?'

His cheerful, if not very tuneful, singing could be heard for a great distance around. Everyone knew that his continual theme was, 'Glory, glory, glory. Praise the Lord for the wonders of his creation.'

Billy's brain was an active one and full of ideas. Sometimes, however, Billy's ideas were not God's ideas and God would stop Billy's enthusiastic plans. This happened one day soon after he became 'happy in the Lord'. On one of his walks he passed a hill called Baldhu. As Billy looked up he thought it would be good to have a place of worship on the top of it. In his mind's eye, he could see crowds of people walking up to the chapel in the Sunday morning sunshine. Excitedly he asked the Lord, 'Shall I build a chapel at Baldhu?' Very soon Billy realised that this was not in God's plan. Although Billy was a little disappointed, he accepted that God's ways were best. God had said 'No' to a chapel at Baldhu, so there was nothing more to be said about it.

Billy often had conversations with his Lord; he also had contact with the devil. In the early days of his Christian life, Satan often came to Billy and tried to tempt him back to his old life. On each occasion, Billy refused to listen.

Billy's testimony at Hicks Mill had stirred the hearts of people. Many of them had known about Billy's life of drunkenness and they were amazed at the transformation in him. They told their friends that Billy Bray, the well-known drunkard, had been saved. Most were overjoyed to hear that news, but some refused to believe that his faith was genuine.

The following Sunday, Billy and his family were among the first to arrive at Hicks Mill.

As Billy and his family came into the chapel everyone turned around. The class leader said, 'It's good to see our friend Billy with us this morning.' Then he looked straight at him and said, 'Brother, will you please come out here and tell us something more about the Lord and his goodness to you.' Billy felt strangely embarrassed as he walked to the front of the chapel. He had listened to others speak of their spiritual experiences and now he was being invited to share his thoughts with these good people. This was amazing: poor, uneducated Billy was being invited to speak in Hicks Mill Chapel.

'I want to tell you about my garden,' said Billy with a rather husky voice. 'I never thought much about my "tatters"[1] before, but the Lord's been talking to me about them. When I take the seed potatoes and bury them in the soil, I always put some good manure with them. We all do that, don't we?'

Billy cleared his throat and looked around him. To his surprise he saw that everyone was paying close attention to his words. It seemed to him as though God was taking over his voice and giving him words to say. He resumed his talk and said, 'I think human beings are a bit like tatters. We are all lying in the ground, but some of us are like those tatters that don't do anything. They just lie there until they wither and die. Do you know, friend, my life has been like that for these twenty-nine years. God could not have said

---

[1] 'Tatters' is Billy's way of saying 'potatoes'.

to me, "Well done, good and faithful servant."[2] All of those years, I was lying in the dark doing nothing but dying. Then one day God's Spirit flooded into my soul and I came alive. I wanted to reach up into the sunlight of God's joy and poke my head out of the black cloak of sin that had wrapped its arms around me. I longed to be useful to God. If my tatters don't grow they just die and are no use to me and my family, but those that turn out a bumper crop, give me and my family great joy and satisfaction. That's what I want my life to be. I want to please God and give him joy in serving him.'

Billy suddenly looked solemn and said, 'But my friend, my tatters and your tatters, grow much better if they've got good, nourishing food to help them. If they are planted in poor soil, without good minerals in it, they will turn out to be weedy plants and give a poor crop.'

A sudden smile lit up Billy's face as he continued. 'We all know that those tatters that are sitting in good, well-rotted manure will give us great big tatters. They're like the corn that Jesus said was planted in good soil. "It produced a crop – such a large crop that it was a hundred, sixty or thirty times what was sown."[3]

'And why do those tatters grow well? It's because of what they feed on. So, friend, you must be sure that you feed on the riches of God's Word. I hear that some

---

[2] See Matthew 25:23
[3] See Matthew 13:8

82

of you read penny novels[4] to tickle your fancy, but I tell you it's only the pure Word of God that will enrich your soul.' He raised his voice and pleaded with the people as he shouted, 'Read the Bible, pray about what you read and practice it in your lives. That's the way to produce a good crop for God's glory.'

Billy stopped, turned to the class leader and whispered anxiously, 'Was that all right?' The leader could hardly see him because his eyes were filled with tears. He stretched out his hand to young Billy and said, 'My dear, dear Brother. The Lord has blessed us so much because of your testimony today. May he continue to use you to explain those truths of the Scriptures, and may God bless you and your family as you serve him.'

Many people wanted to speak to Billy and Joey and their family at the end of that meeting. As they walked home, Joey whispered to her husband, 'My dear, dear husband, I know that the Lord has many great things for you to do.'

---

[4] Penny novels were cheap books whose stories had little spiritual teaching in them.

The First Challenge

Some of the shafts, at the mine where Billy was working at that time, were very deep and liable to flooding. By the end of the week, Billy and the other miners were standing waist deep in water and it was impossible to hack out more rock. In those days mine owners had no concern about the safety of the men; all they wanted was as much tin as possible. If the men became too ill to work or they were drowned, there were always plenty of others who would take their places. Sunday was meant to be a rest day for the miners, but mine owners often used that day to deal with flooding.

At 6 o'clock each Saturday evening one of the men was detailed to start up the steam pump. This sucked the flood water up to the surface. It was then tipped into barrels and loaded on to wagons. These wagons were drawn by horses to a place where the water could be emptied without fear of it going back down into the mine. On Sundays a team of eight men took it in turns to work the pumps and drive the horses. They did this twice; once at 6 o'clock in the morning and again twelve hours later. The power from the pumps was enough to clear all of the water out of the shaft. As they took this duty in turn, no one complained about having to work on their day off once every eight weeks.

As Billy and his family left their cottage one Sunday morning, Joey took Billy's arm and whispered, 'Billy, isn't it your turn to be at the mine today?'

Billy said nothing; he had not forgotten that it was his turn. The fact is that he had already spoken to the Lord about it. Billy knew from God's Word that today was the day to worship the Lord and he accepted this.

Billy smiled contentedly and said, 'It is God's will that I stay here and he has assured me that even though the water will continue to trickle into the mine, it'll do no harm to anyone.'

As soon as they arrived at the chapel, they took their seats to worship the Lord. They had begun to look forward to their chapel days. They loved to sing the old hymns they remembered from their childhood. When it was time for testimonies, Billy was again asked to speak. He loved this opportunity to share with the people some of his recent experiences of the Lord. This time he told them about Cornish fishermen. Everyone who lived there had seen the fishermen sailing out to sea in their frail boats, and they all knew the dangers they faced as they tried to catch enough fish to make a living.

In his simple but clear way, Billy reminded the congregation, 'When those boats go out they don't just stay by the safety of the shore; they launch right out into the deep water. They do so because they know that's where the best fish are. It would be much easier for them if they only sailed a little way from land, but if they did so they would probably only catch a few "tiddlers".' Billy paused and with a penetrating look he said, 'Do you remember the story where Jesus told his disciples to "put out into deep water, and let down the nets for a catch?"[1] Well friends, if you want to get great blessings from the Lord, then you have to work hard at it. God doesn't reward lazy people. You have to push out into the deep waters of your faith. You have to learn to trust God even when life is dangerous.'

Then he explained what he meant. 'If you only read your favourite Bible stories and don't try to understand the deeper truths of the gospel, then you'll be weak and flabby believers and you won't have any strength to fight against the devil when things go badly with you.' He paused and cleared his throat. Looking straight at the people in front of him in a pleading voice he said, 'If you are a feeble Christian who doesn't want to take risks for God, then don't be surprised if the devil comes along and tempts you. If you aren't strong in the Lord[2] and you're not wearing God's armour,[3] then you'll find yourself listening to Satan and you'll end up in a spiritual mess.'

Billy suddenly realised that he was starting to preach instead of telling the people about the Lord's

---

[1] Luke 5:4

[2] See Ephesians 6:10

[3] See Ephesians 6:10-18

goodness during the past week. He glanced over to the class leader to see if he looked cross. He quickly knew that all was well when he received an encouraging nod.

As they walked home Joey said, 'Those were wonderful things that you said in chapel this morning, my love.' She looked straight at her husband and said with confidence, 'I don't think you should worry about missing your turn at the mine today. I'm sure everything will be all right.'

After their meal, they all spent a pleasant afternoon together. After they had sung some hymns, the little ones asked for a story and they all listened as Billy read about how Jesus stilled the storm on the lake[4]. Then they talked about the Lord Jesus and how important it is to obey God's Word.

It was still very dark when Billy set out for the mine early on the next day. Few people looked forward to Mondays, but there would be no money to buy food without hard work. Billy knew that it was his turn to set the pumps working at six o'clock that morning. This was designed to clear the remaining water from the tunnels by the time the men reached them at the beginning of their morning shift. Billy made a good job of it and was certain that the working areas were now dry. There was another mine nearby called 'Wheal Fortune.' 'Wheal' was the Cornish word they used for a mine. It was to this one that Billy walked to that morning. As he arrived there, one of the two captains in charge of those two mines came

[4] See Luke 8:22-25

towards him. He saw that it was Captain Hosken, the one who was the strictest of all of the captains.

He could tell by the look on his face that yesterday's absence had been noticed.

'Mr Bray,' bellowed Captain Hosken in a very harsh tone. 'Where were you yesterday? You were supposed to be here pumping out the mine at 6 a.m. and again at 6 p.m. Speak up lad. Why didn't you come?'

In a clear, but quiet voice, he said, 'It wasn't the Lord's will that I should come.'

As soon as Billy said that, the face of the Captain turned purple. He stood there for a moment and then shouted, 'I'll "Lord's will" you. I'm the boss here and you will obey me or get out.' Then he stopped and turned around. In a much lower tone he said, 'You may be a good worker, Bray, but I want you out of this mine – and I want you to go right now. I won't have you working here anymore. Get out, and stay out.'

As he stalked away, the Lord spoke to Billy's heart and said, 'You have me as your friend and I am the Lord of the rocks and the mountains. Don't be afraid because I am with you whatever happens.'

In a quiet tone, Billy called after his captain and said, 'Mr Hosken, you have to understand that I have a new Master now. He has told me that because he is my Rock then I can chase a thousand or put two thousand to flight'[5].

As he walked away, he knew that Joey would complain because now they would have no money and

---

[5] See Deuteronomy 32:30

she needed to buy food and clothes for the children. He, too, was concerned about how they would buy food, but he did not feel unduly cast down. He even started to whistle as he walked away. However, he had not gone far when he heard a noise behind him. He turned and saw that it was his mate, William Roberts. 'Whatever is the matter with you, my friend?' exclaimed Billy. William looked as though he had been crying. Billy waited until he caught him up. His face was very sad as he blurted out, 'Billy, what shall I do? I have a wife and children to look after, Captain Hosken has also turned me out of his mine.'

William looked as if he was going to burst into tears again. Looking straight at Billy he said, 'I don't want to hurt you, my friend, but I've got to say this. Billy, it wasn't my fault that you didn't go to the pumps yesterday, but because you didn't go, I have also been dismissed.'

Billy then realised how our actions can affect other people. He knew he belonged to Jesus, yet his good friend was suffering because he had refused to work on Sundays. As they both regained their composure, Billy gently laid his hand on William Roberts' arm. With a loud and very firm voice he said, 'No. You will not be turned away because of me. You cannot be blamed because I did not carry out my duty. Let us go back to the mine and I will talk to Captain Hosken and try to persuade him to give you back your job.'

They walked up to the head of the mine. Billy had been praying all the way and asked the Lord to help him get his friend's job back. They knocked on the office door politely and heard someone say, 'Come in.' Captain Hosken looked up as they entered and said, 'Oh. It's you two.'

'Sir,' said Billy, 'Please do not dismiss my mate, William Roberts. He's a good man and it wasn't his fault that I stayed in chapel yesterday, instead of manning the pumps.'

In a much calmer tone the Captain looked at Billy and said, 'As I said earlier, you are a very good worker, Billy, and I don't want to lose you, but the fact is that everyone must take their turn at pumping the water on Sundays. After all it only happens once every eight weeks, so what is wrong with that?'

Billy knew that he must stand his ground. With a polite, but firm, tone Billy looked at the Captain and said, 'You know, sir, that I have a new Master, and he's a good one too, praise his holy name. He tells me that I must not work on the Sabbath Day, but keep it holy.' Then, before he could stop himself, he added, 'I shall do as he tells me, by his help, and I shall not work any more on the Sabbath Day.'

'Help me Lord,' Billy prayed silently in his mind. God did help him, and the aid came from an unexpected quarter. No sooner had Billy finished his speech than Mr Mitchel, the clerk sitting at his desk in the corner of the room, quietly said, 'If I felt like William Bray then I wouldn't work on the Sabbath Day either.'

There was a sudden hush in the room and everyone looked at the Captain to see what he would do. It seemed an age before the silence was broken. The Captain looked strangely uncomfortable and in a more pleasant tone said, 'You can both work here if you want to.'

William smiled and looked very relieved, but Billy said, 'That's no good because I can't work here on Sundays. I can only be here if you give me other work that doesn't involve Sundays.'

The Captain looked at Billy and said, 'Yes, I have other work as it happens. You can go to that engine by the power house and wheel away the ashes from the spent fuel, if that would suit you.'

It was Billy's turn to look relieved and he replied, 'Thank you very much, sir. I will now be able to go to the meetings on Sundays and to the preaching services in the evenings as well.'

So, for Billy there would be no more Sunday working and no more shift work. He would just do the morning and the afternoon sessions. He was very pleased, because he could now serve the Lord as he wished. All he had to do was to go and tell Joey that he would be free in the evenings, but as a consequence his wage packet would be very much smaller. As he walked home, he wondered what she would have to say about that!

Revival

Early the next morning, Billy took a wheelbarrow to the engine room. There he found several men who were already at work. One team cleared the ashes, which had come from the fires that drove the engine room pumps. Another shovelled those ashes into the barrows and a third group wheeled them to a place some distance from the mine head. Everyone was very busy. Billy joined the men who removed the ash away from the engine room.

'What are you doing here, Billy?' said one of them. 'We all thought that Captain Hosken had forbidden you to work here anymore.'

Billy smiled and then told them the whole story. As they were talking, Billy felt a wonderful sense of God's power coming over him. He told his workmate about how he and William had got their jobs back. The other man looked surprised and said, 'That was lucky.'

'Luck didn't come into it, my friend,' said Billy. 'It was the Lord who heard my prayer and he softened the Captain's heart.'

Now they were all listening. Billy looked at each in turn and said, 'You see, it all worked out well in the end. This is because the Lord always honours those who honour him.'[1]

Once again Billy stooped, picked up the handles of his barrow and resumed his work. As he wheeled his load away he called out, 'I told Captain Hosken that work on the surface would suit me, because then I could go to chapel every Sunday.'

As he returned for a fresh load of ash, a quiet voice said, 'Good for you Billy, I always admire those who do what God tells them.'

When Billy turned to give his new mate a smile of thanks, he noticed something was wrong. As he said, 'What's the matter friend?' the other man fell down in the dust at Billy's feet and started to sob. In a very loud voice he cried out, 'Lord have mercy on me. I know I'm a sinner and I need your forgiveness.'

Billy quickly put down his barrow and knelt down beside him and told him, 'Our God is a merciful God and he longs to forgive. Do you know that he has promised to wash away our sins, if we are truly sorry and are determined to turn away from them?'

As Billy said this, his new friend became calmer and said, 'Thank you Lord, for saving my soul.' Joy overwhelmed Billy's whole being as he saw another person come home to God. The man then explained to him that he attended Twelveheads Methodist Chapel. 'You know the one, Billy? I think your grandfather used to take you there as a child.'

---

[1] See 1 Samuel 2:30

Twelveheads Chapel was no further from Billy's home than Hicks Mill Chapel, but Billy had not gone there because he felt their services were far too formal.

The next time he came face to face with his new Christian friend, Billy asked him, 'How are things at Twelveheads Chapel?'

With a lowered voice filled with wonder, his friend said, 'I'm told that the Spirit of God is moving there, and many people are calling upon him for mercy.' For a second, his friend looked sad and then continued, 'I tried very hard to seek the Lord, but nothing happened. I was just thinking about it when you told us about how God had helped you with your job. It was then that I thought to myself, "If God can work for Billy, then he can work in my life too."'

Anyone who was walking on the pathway that led from the mine to Billy's cottage would have smiled that night. This was because, as Billy trudged his way home, he sang at the top of his voice, 'Glory, glory, glory, praise the Lord.' As soon as he arrived indoors and had kissed Joey and the children he announced, 'There is revival going on at Twelveheads Chapel and I believe the Lord wants me to go there instead of working at the mine.'

He had wondered what his wife would say when he told her that he would not be earning any money for the next few days. He need not have worried, as Joey gave him a big hug and said, 'My dear, dear Billy.

If the Lord has called you to do this then I am pleased. Don't worry about me and the children. I shall stay at home with them and pray that God will help you in this wonderful work.'

When Billy arrived at Twelveheads Methodist Chapel, the meeting had already started. Instead of the dull singing and the tedious prayers, he was greeted by a loud din. Some of the people were shouting 'Praise the Lord' and others were weeping. As soon as Billy shut the chapel door behind him, a young man came up to him and said, 'Mr Bray, there is someone crying over there. Please will you go and speak to him.' Billy, elated by the power of the Holy Spirit, knelt down next to the man who was in distress. Billy immediately gave an enormous shout of 'Glory, glory, glory. Praise the Lord for his goodness and favour to us all.' He half expected to hear loud whispers of 'Be quiet. This is the house of the Lord!' but none came. Instead he heard cheerful voices say, 'Bless you my brother.'

As soon as Billy's shout had left his lips, the young man fell forward on to his knees. With a loud and unashamed cry he called on the Lord to have mercy on his soul. As soon as this happened, several other people began to fill the chapel with agonising cries of longing.

Every day for the rest of the week, more and more called on the Lord for salvation. This was Billy's first experience of revival.

By the Friday evening of that week, there were even more people rejoicing in the Lord's salvation. Every evening, Billy had arrived home very tired, but exhilarated by the wonderful experience of the Lord's goodness.

Instead of going to the mine each morning, Billy made his way to Twelveheads Chapel. There were always people coming and going, and many of them went away rejoicing in their new-found salvation. For the whole of that Friday, Billy spoke and prayed with many seeking souls. He quickly gained experience of standing up and addressing large groups of people. Although he earned no money, that week's work was very profitable. It was to be the beginning of his fruitful ministry for the Lord, not just at Twelveheads but throughout Cornwall and beyond.

Towards the end of the afternoon, there came a period of silence; the chapel was empty. It was then that Billy thought about Joey and the children. She had been talking to him about their lack of money. In his mind he could still hear her voice ringing in his ears, 'You ought to go and earn some money, Billy.'

While he was considering this, a thought came to him. 'It's Friday evening and I do believe this is the Friday which is taking-on day.' None of the miners had permanent jobs. They all had to go to the mine on a certain day (called 'taking-on day') and there they bid for work. That Friday was when the new contracts were allocated. Billy wondered whether he should go to the mine and try and get work.

As soon as those words passed through his mind, another thought hit him. 'But, I am working here and the Lord is blessing my labours in this chapel.' Billy knew that God had given him his dear wife and lovely children, but he also knew he had promised 'to meet all his needs according to his glorious riches in Christ Jesus.'[2] Joey was sure that the work of the Lord must take first place in Billy's life, but he did not take his responsibility to his family lightly.

He fell on his knees to thank the Lord for all his goodness and for using him in his service. At that moment he heard the door open. It was the polite young man from the chapel and he was walking towards the seat where Billy was praying. 'Excuse me Mr Bray' he said. 'There are several men here from the mine and they want to see you urgently.'

As Billy rose up from his knees and walked over to his colleagues, he wondered if he was in more trouble. He was even more puzzled, when he saw the look on their faces.

'We have work for you Billy,' said one of the men. Billy looked surprised. He was grateful that the men had taken the trouble to come and tell him about the opportunity to earn some money. The children had been complaining about feeling hungry, so he would be glad of some money to buy them food.

---

[2] See Philippians 4:19

'Thanks for coming lads, but I have already told Captain Hosken that I won't work in the mines on Sundays.'

One of the men grinned and had a chuckle in his voice, 'Who said anything about having to work on Sundays? There's a new mine opened at Chapels Shaft. It's twenty metres deeper than it used to be. Although it has the usual problem of loads of water coming into it, they keep the pumps working the whole time we are down there. This means that it's not necessary for anyone to go to that particular mine on the Sabbath Day.'

'But Captain Hosken said he wouldn't let me work underground anymore,' Billy declared. But as it turned out, it was Captain Hosken himself who had asked for Billy to come back. It was several minutes before Billy said anything. He was quietly talking it over with his Lord. 'This is a wonderful provision of the Lord, lads. I hadn't said anything to anyone, not even Joey, but I was beginning to wonder how we were going to manage. This just goes to show that those who have the Lord as their shepherd lack nothing, because he is their provider.'

He looked directly at the man who had brought him the news of work. 'My friend, is the Lord your Shepherd? Can you honestly say, "The Lord is MY Shepherd. I shall not be in want?"'[3]

That evening his little cottage rang for joy. Even the children squealed with delight when they saw the happiness on the faces of their parents.

---

[3] Psalm 23:1

Later, Joey put the youngsters to bed and Billy read a Bible story to them. When the youngsters were settled, Billy and Joey sat down to talk over the events of the day. Joey was always careful not to say anything that might dampen her husband's enthusiasm. However, she realised that she must tell her husband what was on her mind.

With great tenderness, Joey asked, 'How could Captain Hosken change his mind so quickly?' She looked at Billy for any sign that he disapproved of her lack of faith, but he nodded for her to continue. 'Are you sure you won't have to work on the Lord's Day?' Billy's face shone with joy as he answered, 'Well, that's what the men said and I believe them. After all the Lord can do far more than "all we ask or imagine, according to his power that is at work within us."'[4]

That weekend was a joyful one. On the Sunday morning, the whole family set off to walk once more to Twelveheads Chapel. During the service, a good many people came to know the Lord as their Saviour and the ceiling rang with the praises of God's people.

A few weeks later, things started to return to the normal chapel routine. However, the exciting events of that week's revival would be talked about for many years. No longer did people attend that chapel on Sundays because it was the respectable thing to do; they now went because they knew and loved the Lord.

---

[4] Ephesians 3:20

They delighted to sing his praises and listen to the teaching of the Bible.

As the revival was over, Billy realised that he must go back to his own chapel at Hicks Mill. He also went back to work. Although work at Chapel Shaft was demanding, it was also very rewarding. When Billy counted his wages at the end of the month he found out that he had earned far more than he imagined would be possible. He was certainly taking home more money now that he wasn't drinking it away. As he hurried home his cheery voice echoed round the hills.

Billy's singing was still rather tuneless, but at least it was full of praise to God. It could be heard a long time before he reached home. That particular day, the door of the cottage burst open and Billy entered the house dancing and singing, 'Glory, glory, glory to the Lord for he has counted me "worthy of double honour."'[5]

'Sit down Billy; sit down,' said Joey with a big smile, but Billy continued to sing and dance around the room. 'Billy, Billy, Billy,' said his wife, 'how are we going to rejoice unless you tell us what the Lord has done?'

Billy hugged Joey and exclaimed, 'My dear, dear wife, do you remember how much I was paid for working in that mine where I was expected to work on the Lord's Day?'

'I remember,' said Joey. Of course she did! She'd had to try to make that money stretch to buying the

---

[5] See 1 Timothy 5:17

food and clothes they needed. In a matter of fact tone she said, 'you got two pounds a month, dear.'

With a twinkle in his eye, Billy looked up at her and said, 'Well, my sweet darling, the Lord has now given us three pounds – every month.'

The children had been straining their ears to catch the conversation. They jumped as their mother screeched with delight. Billy's voice rang out with loud praise as he sang,

> It is a heaven below, our Jesus to know;
> And while we do his blessed will,
> We bear our heaven about us still.[6]

When Billy arrived at work the next day, he was still feeling ecstatic. He sang even louder than usual as he climbed down the rickety ladders. When he reached the end of the last one he stood and waited for his seven companions to join him. That day it was Billy's turn to help the men decide where each pair should work. Before they started, Billy said, 'My friends, let's ask the Lord's blessing on our labours today!' Billy prayed and, as usual, prayed that if any should die that day, that it would be him.

Billy and his mate, who was a man of his own age, were to work at the very lowest depth that day. After they had reached the rough platform at the end of the shaft they decided to make another tunnel. This one was to be in a slightly upward direction. 'Let's pray,

[6] Quoted by Chris Wright, p.57, but I have been unable to trace the source of this hymn.

friend, that if we dig a new shaft here, we will find many rich seams of tin ore in it.'

While Billy hacked the rock away to make the new tunnel, his mate worked away behind him. It was not easy because the water nearly rose waist high. 'It's not very nice down here,' said his companion.

'Never mind friend,' said Billy. 'I believe the Lord is going to give us good fortune in this place.' His companion was already used to Billy's quotations from the Bible so he chuckled silently as he heard him say, 'If the Lord would save Sodom and Gomorrah for ten righteous, then he will give us a dry tunnel for the two of us to work in.'[7]

At the moment Billy said those words, his companion lifted his pick high in the air and drove it hard into the ground and they heard a sudden loud gurgling noise. They looked in amazement as the water fell away leaving them standing on ground that was completely free from water. Billy whooped for joy and said, 'You see, my friend, the Lord can work miracles today, just as he did in the days of old. He is the same Lord, and there are no limits to his power. Bless his holy name.'

Because they could now see where they were standing, they started to make a flat place where they could put the newly cut rocks. The boys working with them could then come and take it away, while Billy and his mate did the much harder work of cutting out more rock.

---

[7] Taken from Genesis 18:32

Sometimes the Lord spoke very clearly to Billy, even though there wasn't an audible voice to be heard. Sometimes God moved in Billy's heart without him being conscious of words.

As they continued to work, Billy experienced an overwhelming desire to move out of their cramped position. 'We need to go back down there friend, and pray,' said Billy. So they started to edge their way back to where they could stand in a more upright position.

Just as Billy and his companion got down on their knees, there was a deafening noise and dust filled the air. They hurried back and were horrified at the sight that met their eyes. Instead of their new tunnel there was now a huge pile of rocks. Billy reckoned that about one ton of it had fallen on the very place where they had just been working.

Billy knew that his friend was not a real Christian so he said, 'If the stones had fallen on me I should be in heaven by now, but what about you? Where would you have been?'

Then he prayed, in a very loud voice, 'Lord, have you saved me because there is more work for me to do?'

Eventually his companion found enough breath to speak, 'Billy, what made you move us away to pray just then?'

'It was the prompting of the Lord, my friend,' Billy replied. 'He's good and he doesn't want even one sinner to die. He would rather they repented of their sins, and came to Christ to be saved.'[8] Billy spoke in hushed tones to his friend. He looked straight at him and said, 'We have just been saved from death, so why don't you seek the Lord while he can be found. Why don't you call upon him while he is near?'[9]

As Billy trudged his way home later that evening, he thanked the Lord for his guidance and for his help in witnessing to his grace.

As he was speaking to the Lord, the devil tempted Billy. Billy thought he heard God say, 'Billy Bray, you'll be a great man.' He was about to respond with, 'Thank you Lord,' when a thought hit him. He remembered what John the Baptist had said of the Lord Jesus, 'He must become greater; I must become less.'[10]

As he journeyed home, he thought more about this. A huge number of birds jumped up from their roosting and flew into the air in fright as he shouted, 'Nonsense. It's not Billy Bray who will be great; but the Lord. Praise his glorious name.'

He knew that the devil would tempt him in all kinds of ways. 'I must take care,' he said to himself. 'If God is going to use me to lead sinners to Christ, I must remain humble and remember that salvation comes only from the Lord[11] not from Billy Bray.

---

[8] See 2 Peter 3:9
[9] See Isaiah 55:6
[10] John 3:30
[11] See Jonah 2:9

Billy's Life of Abstinence

Everywhere he went, Billy told people that he had been made happy in Jesus and he urged them to seek the Lord too. He was not satisfied when people said, 'I'm a Christian. I go to church every Sunday and put money in the collection plate.' His usual reply to that was, 'But what about your soul? You give your money to the Lord, but have you given your life to Christ?'

One day on his way home from church, the Lord spoke to Billy's heart and said, 'Fast this day for my sake.' Billy did not ask why he should abstain from food, but from that day on he did not eat anything on Sundays until around 4 p.m.

Many of his Christian friends were worried about his fasting. He worked extremely hard during the week and Sunday was the only day he did not go to the mines. 'You need to build up your strength,' said one of his friends. 'The devil is trying to starve you because he knows that the Lord wants to use you for his glory. Please stop this nonsense and eat heartily on Sundays because you have much preaching to do.'

Billy smiled at his friend because he knew he was concerned for his health. 'I'll tell you what I'll do,' said Billy. 'I will ask the Lord and he will let me know whether I should continue to fast every Lord's Day.'

The next Sunday, Billy rose early and left his wife and children in bed. He came down stairs, knelt and poured out his heart in prayer, 'Lord, you know what the people are saying, how I shall starve myself. Now, my dear Lord, if I must eat meat then tell me to do so.' After he had finished he got up from his knees, sat on a stool and waited, but nothing happened. He felt no different from before and so he prayed again, 'Lord, should I fast?'

As soon as he asked a second time, the power of God fell on him so that he nearly ended up on the floor. He steadied himself, smiled triumphantly and said, 'I don't care what my friends say because now I am certain that it is your will that I should continue to fast on Sundays.'

Billy did not talk to others much about his fasting as he did not look for praise from men. Billy's reasoning for this was that Jesus had said, 'When you fast, do not look sombre as the hypocrites do, for they disfigure their faces to show men they are fasting. I tell you the truth; they have received their reward in full.'[1]

Soon after his conversion, Billy was convicted by the Holy Spirit about his habit of smoking. 'I'd rather go down the mine without my dinner than without my pipe,' he used to tell his friends. He not only smoked his pipe; he chewed tobacco as well.

---

[1] Matthew 6:16

It was not long after he had spoken up at the class meeting, that he began to wonder whether it was wrong to smoke his pipe. He was not singing as he walked home from the mine that day, because he was listening to the still small voice of his God. As he reached for his pipe, the Holy Spirit convicted Billy clearly. Billy realised that God was showing him how he had made an idol of his pipe. 'You are lusting after an idol, just like the Israelites in days of old. I want you to give it up and worship me with your whole heart.'

Billy stood still on the path and raised his pipe to his lips. It had always helped him to think before, but this time God's words shouted into his soul, 'Worship me with clean lips.'[2] This filled him with awe and he remembered a recent visit to his friend, Mary Hook. She had asked him whether he felt guilty about his smoking habit. He told her that he had been wondering whether he was making an idol of his pipe. Very quickly she whispered to him, 'It's the Lord who is telling you that.'

As soon as he arrived home, he walked straight to the fire place. Joey looked up in surprise because he usually kissed her before he did anything else. She wondered what her husband was going to do and she watched as he stood in front of the fire, took his bag of tobacco out of his pocket and threw it into the flames. It spluttered for a moment and then burned away with a bluish flame.

---

[2] See Matthew 15:8

Joey was speechless, because she knew how much Billy's pipe meant to him. In amazement, she watched as he put his hand into his pocket once again and took out his well-loved pipe. He threw it on the floor and crushed it with his foot, saying, 'Ashes to ashes and dust to dust.'[3]

Joey rushed up to him and threw her arms around his neck. 'My dear, dear husband, what you have just done was a very brave thing.' Billy turned to her and smiled, 'My darling wife; I have to obey the Lord.'

While the meal was being prepared, Billy sat on his stool and thought about the events of the day. He stretched his hand into his pocket and suddenly pulled it away again. The pipe had gone and so had his favourite pastime. 'Wouldn't you like to have had a draw on your pipe,' said a voice in his head. The youngest child squealed as Billy jumped to his feet and shouted at the top of his voice, 'Get behind me, Satan.'[4]

Billy never smoked again for the rest of his life. Every future time the temptation came to him to smoke, he asked his Lord, 'Please keep the thought of smoking out of my mind. Give me strength to stop this habit and help me.'

One Sunday the minister responsible for Hicks Mill, arrived to take the morning service. Because he also had the care of many other chapels, he only came to each chapel every month or so. As

---

[3] This phrase is used in funeral services and is based on Genesis 3:19.
[4] See Matthew 16:23

he preached, Billy added his own hearty 'Amen' at regular intervals. The minister had to preach at the afternoon service at another chapel, but before he left he walked over to Billy and said, 'How are you this fine morning?'

'I'm well sir, praise the Lord,' answered Billy.

As the minister sat and talked, Billy realised that this was to be no ordinary chat. 'I've been hearing about the way the Lord is using you Billy and I want to ask you if you would be willing to go on the plan.'

'I've heard of it sir, but what would I have to do if I went on the plan?'

The minister sat down next to him and explained, 'You know about the Methodist chapels, where you grew up. Well, they all have to share their minister with other preaching places. Obviously, he can't preach in all of them at the same time so that's why local preachers have been appointed to take the services in these other chapels. We do the same in our chapels.'

Billy already knew that Hicks Mill Chapel was linked with many others, but he was startled when the minister said, 'I believe God is calling you Billy, to join those who go from place to place to preach the Word of God.'

Billy managed to stutter out, 'Sir, I'm only a poor tin miner. I've got no education or book-learning.' He quickly added, 'I can read my Bible and I know my hymn book, but what use would I be to anyone?'

The minister threw his head back and uttered a long, powerful guffaw. Eventually he calmed down and said, 'I'm sorry Billy, but that's so funny. The Lord has already been using you to lead so many sinners to Christ, and you ask me, "What use would I be?" In a more confidential tone he added, 'I know about the good work you did at Twelveheads and your witness to your fellow miners. What is even more important is that the Lord knows too. God is now calling you to stand up and preach the gospel.'

Billy needed no more convincing. He realised that it was not the minister who was calling him to preach; it was the dear Lord himself. He did not have the money, nor could he spare the time to be specially trained to be a preacher. But if the Lord could call Peter, James and John to serve him, and they were only fishermen, then he could call poor Billy Bray to do the same thing.

He heard the minister's voice break through his jumbled thoughts. 'Please pray about this Billy, and let me know what you decide.'

Billy again looked worried. 'Before you go, sir, there's one thing that worries me. I don't think I know how to write out a sermon.'

The preacher patted Billy on his shoulder and said, 'The Lord will give you the words to say.' With that the preacher left the building.

Billy knew that several of the chapels were some distance from his home. He had no horse to ride, nor did he know anyone who would lend him one. This meant that he would have to walk everywhere.

Billy then shouted out at the top of his voice, 'I'm going to walk all over south west Cornwall and preach the gospel to every person I see, praise the Lord for his great name.'

Billy hurried home to tell Joey the news. As soon as he opened the door he shouted, 'Joey dear, the dear Lord has called your husband to be an evangelist.'

Some wives would have been upset by the thought that their husband was going to spend Sundays away from home, but Joey beamed with pleasure. They spent the rest of that evening talking about how Billy could go about his task.

After his work that Saturday morning, he took his Bible and hymn book and went up into the bedroom to prepare his message for the next day. At the top of a piece of paper he wrote, 'Sermon.' Then he sat back and thought, and then he thought some more. A sad feeling came over him and he put the pencil down. The only thing he had written on the paper was the word, 'Sermon.'

'The preacher said to me, "Billy, the Lord will give you the words to say."'

So, instead of writing notes, Billy spent the afternoon reading his Bible and hymn book and then speaking the matter over with his God. After several hours, Joey heard his footsteps and he climbed down the stairs to eat his evening meal. 'The Lord has given me a good time of meditating on his Word. I am going to open my mouth and the Lord has promised to fill it with good things of the gospel.'

Early that Sunday morning he set off, having brushed his old coat and put on his hat. He knew that chapel was about nine miles away from his home, but the distance seemed to fly by as he talked with his Lord along the way.

For Billy, that Sunday was the start of a life-time of preaching the gospel. Most preachers arrived at chapel with a well-prepared set of sermon notes, but the only thing that Billy carried into the pulpit was his Bible. He just stood up, prayed and then opened his mouth to speak, but he was not unprepared. His heart and his mind were well equipped to speak of the glories of the gospel. His words were not grand and eloquent; they were just plain and to the point.

As he spoke, God broke into the lives of those who heard him and before his first sermon was over, several people were on their knees crying out for the Lord to have mercy on their souls.

Soon after his first sermon, it was not unusual for large numbers of people to walk long distances to hear him. When he saw a congregation crowding into the chapel he would start by saying, 'I do hope you haven't come to hear poor Billy Bray preach; I trust you've come to hear the voice of the Saviour calling you to follow him.'

Like everyone else, Billy wore his Sunday best clothes on the Lord's Day, but they were very drab and their old material was filled with patches. Billy simply had no spare cash to buy the sort of clothes people expected a preacher to wear.

As he set out each Sunday morning, he could tell by the look on Joey's face that she was a little ashamed of his appearance. However, every spare penny he earned was needed to provide for the family.

Often the paths were muddy and he would arrive at the chapel rain-spattered, with dirty streaks down his trousers. It was not unusual for him to preach three times on a Sunday, and each time in a different place. On some days, he had walked twenty miles by the time he returned home.

As he passed a friend's house one Sunday morning, the man called out, 'Why do you go to preach wearing that old thick cotton jacket?'

Billy smiled and replied, 'I wear it because it's my best one.' Then he added, with an even broader grin, 'Would you want me to go to chapel in my torn working clothes?' In case he had given offence to his friend, he quickly added, 'The dear Lord gave me power to do his will, and my poor clothes don't keep me at home. These are far, far better than I ought to wear because I deserve to be down in hell fire with the devil and his angels.'

When his friend heard this, he shook him warmly by the hand and said, 'Well, God bless you my friend, and may he continue to use you for his glory – whatever clothes you are wearing.'

For many months, Billy spent every Sunday walking to the chapels at Flushing, Penryn, Falmouth and even to Cambourne, which was on the northern coast of Cornwall. Gradually, he was invited to preach in chapels that were even further away. He never worried about how far he had to walk; his only concern was to do God's will and be able to point men, women and children to Christ, who had saved him from the flames of hell.

Although he arrived back home tired and dishevelled each Sunday evening, he always had a cheery smile and warm kiss for his Joey. On his return one Sunday, she opened the door and was very surprised. Instead of his old jacket, Billy stood on the doorstep in a splendid jacket. Underneath it was a waist coat. With her eyes opened wide she said, 'My, you look like a real gentleman now. Where did you get those things?'

'The Lord provided them,' said Billy and then he told Joey the whole story. The previous Sunday while he was walking along, a servant girl joined him on the way to Falmouth. When she discovered that he was a preacher of the gospel she asked him if he was wearing his 'Sunday best'. He explained that he only had two coats and as the other was used for mining, the one he was wearing was his best one.

'Do you know, Joey, I never thought any more about it, although I did tell the girl that I was pleased that she knew the Lord as her Saviour. When I passed that same way this morning, the same girl stood there carrying this smart coat and waist coat. She told me that the Lord had put it in her heart to get me a warmer coat and that she'd told a good man who belonged to the Quakers[5] about our conversation the previous Sunday. That sweet, kind girl asked this man if he had a spare coat that could be given to me.

'Apparently he had no spare coat, but after he thought about it for a moment he took off the one he was wearing – and the waist coat – and said, "Give these to Mr Bray, with my blessing."'

Joey wanted to know the name of the kind man, but Billy did not know it. He was to experience the same sort of kindness throughout the rest of his life. Not only did Quaker friends give him clothes to wear; they also supplied clothes and blankets for the children. He never had to buy new shoes either, because these friends supplied new ones when his old ones had worn thin.

As the months past, the Lord also provided for Billy in other ways. It had become his habit to eat no food after Saturday evening until the evening of Sunday. However, people were very kind to him and after the service, many would wish to entertain him for a good

---

[5] Quakers are members of The Religious Society of Friends, a Christian movement founded by George Fox in England about 1650.

meal. It became his habit to accept the first invitation that was offered, even if that person only had a very poor home. When he arrived there, he always refused food, even though some of the homes he went to offered far richer food than he had at home. 'I thank you kindly my friend,' he would say, 'but all that I need this day is to feast on the Word of God.' However, he often sat down with his host and drank a cup of tea with them. Then he would be on his way again.

On one particular Sunday morning, he was due to preach at Flushing for the 10.30 service. It was a nine mile walk to the chapel, but he was pleased to do so. In the afternoon he wanted to go and hear a certain Mr Tregaskis, who was due to preach a few miles away, at Penryn. On the way there, Billy took his copy of the preaching plan out of his pocket and, to his horror, found out that he was due to preach at Mylor Bridge at half past two that afternoon. As it was nearly time for the service to start he ran all the way. He smiled and thought, 'I used to run in the devil's service; now I must run in the Lord's service.'

When he arrived, puffing and blowing, twenty minutes after the service was due to start, he saw a crowd outside the chapel; they were all waiting for him to arrive. He got his breath back while the congregation sang the first hymn. Even though the service was late in starting, everyone had a joyful time. Throughout the whole afternoon there were many calls of 'praise the Lord'.

Billy the Chapel Builder

Not everyone welcomed Billy when he preached at their chapel. Some complained about his rough manner and it became obvious that they were jealous of his success in winning people for Christ. However, Billy's response was, 'It's not Billy who saves people, nor is it Billy's preaching, it's the precious blood of Christ that washes away their sin.' Yet even Billy's gentle words did not satisfy some of the people and they continued to grumble against him even though he treated them kindly.

Billy remained on friendly terms with the members of the Methodist Chapel at Twelveheads, but he was troubled because there were large areas of his part of Cornwall that had no Bible preaching. One day as he was walking in the direction of Baldhu, he passed a stamp house. This had once been used to smash the ore so that any tin could be extracted. A dozen or more people met there each Sunday for a class meeting. Billy took a look inside and saw that it was damp and dreary and not a place to take people to hear the preaching of the gospel.

As he was thinking about this, he felt as though God was prompting him to something. 'Billy, build me a preaching house at Cross Lanes.' This was something quite new. He was to build a chapel where the gospel could be preached.

Billy continued to think about this as he went about his work down the mine, and as he walked around the countryside. When he spoke to Joey about it she said, 'Billy, how are you going to build a chapel on your own? You spend every Sunday preaching and travelling around the area. You have a family to look after. When will you have time to build a chapel?'

Billy replied, 'Time belongs to the Lord. If it is his will, then he will give the money, the strength and the time to do it.'

Billy was not only a good husband and father, but he was also a faithful son. Although his mother had sent him to stay with his grandfather when his father died, he never thought badly of her. On his next visit to her home, he chatted about God's plan for a chapel at Cross Lanes. Then he became excited when he saw his mother's eyes light up. 'Billy, I've got a small piece of land in that area. I could give it to you, so you can build your chapel there.'

'Mother, my own dear mother,' said Billy, throwing his arms around her neck. 'You're God's answer to the problem I've been wrestling with. I had no idea how I could buy a piece of land for a chapel.'

Billy's mother laughed as she disentangled her son's arms from around her neck and said, 'I'll gladly give it son, if that's what you want.' Billy suddenly looked more serious. 'It's not what I want; it's what God wants – and I'll make sure that he gets it too.'

As Billy hurried home, his mind worked overtime. He could visualise the chapel taking shape and crowds of people coming into it. He imagined he could hear the walls of the chapel echoing with the voice of the preacher as he proclaimed the good news of salvation.

He burst in through the door when he arrived home and shouted, 'Joey, Joey, the Lord is answering our desires. He's given us a piece of land where we can build the chapel.' They sat down together and talked about who they could ask to help them.

The next day he was not due to work until the afternoon shift, so early in the morning he took some tools from his garden and hurried over to the plot of land his mother had given him. An old hedge went round most of it, but this did not deter Billy. He set to work and quickly uprooted it, piece by piece. He did not give up. What Billy lacked in height, he made up for in strength. A few stubborn bushes with very deep roots would not deter him from his mission. Before the morning was out he had cleared the whole area and had started to put in markers where the foundations would be.

Digging into the stony ground was very hard work, but as Billy stooped to clear away the soil he had removed, he started to make music. If anyone had been passing by that morning, they would have heard the clank of his spade on the hard ground and his cracked voice singing,

> There is a land of pure delight,
> where saints immortal reign;
> Infinite day excludes the night,
> And pleasures banish pain.[1]

Every time he had a few spare hours, he returned and continued to prepare the ground for the new chapel. Each Sunday, he reminded his congregation about the needs of this new chapel. Many of the Bible Christians promised to pray for him in his work. Others offered their advice, but a small number came and assisted him with the heavy work of moving the soil. He had assumed that the people who held their class meeting in the stamp house would be excited about the new chapel.

However, he was wrong about the Stamp House crowd. They not only failed to come and help with the work, but most of them turned against him. They even tried to get their minister to be hostile towards Billy's Chapel. Despite the opposition, there were a few who came and helped with the hard physical work of preparing the ground. One day one of them said, 'Billy, I'm sorry that those others at the class meeting are against you. Do you want me to go and speak to them and tell them how wrong they are?'

'No,' said Billy. 'Leave them alone. St Paul had his thorn in the flesh, but he discovered that God gave

---

[1] Hymn 649 Isaac Watts.

him grace to cope with it,[2] so I must learn to build this chapel for God's glory without their help.'

After some weeks of energetic activity, enough ground had been cleared to lay a level foundation stone for the chapel. He invited those who had supported him to meet with him for the first 'preaching' that was to be held there. The crowd was not great, but this did not upset Billy.

Billy drew a deep breath and said, 'If this new chapel, which they say is to be called Bethel, stands for one hundred years and one soul is converted in it every year, that will bring one hundred to salvation – and one soul is worth more than the whole of Cornwall.'

He then danced on the stone and shouted, 'Glory, glory, bless the Lord!' Following this excited gesture, he launched into his sermon and was encouraged by the many shouts of 'Hallelujah, praise the Lord' from those who were present on that auspicious day.

The work of building Bethel Chapel was slow. Ordinary people like Billy did most of the physical work, but money was needed to buy building materials like wood and stones. Some people gave Billy money for these items, but the most a working man could earn in those days was ten shillings a week. When the mines only produced small quantities of tin, the wages were lower still.

[2] See 2 Corinthians 12:7-10

This meant that much of the money given to Billy for the chapel was in pennies, half-pennies and even farthings. A farthing was one quarter of a penny.

Many friends contributed to the building fund and Billy added to it every spare penny he earned. Before very long there was one pound and fifteen shillings available for him to buy materials. Billy assumed that his friends at the class meeting would be as excited as he was, but he was wrong. Several of them raised objections to Billy's Chapel. They agreed that a new chapel should be built, but they questioned why it should be at Cross Lanes. Some of them felt that it should be built at Twelveheads and others thought that Tippets Stamps was where there was a greater need.

Knowing the way tin miners talked, Billy took little notice of their grumbling until the minister responsible for that area visited him. 'Billy,' he said, 'the men feel you are rushing ahead too quickly with your new chapel. Some of them are saying that there is a better place to build it.'

Billy was always very respectful of the minister and accepted his spiritual authority, but he was upset by the way this conversation was going. 'Sir,' he said, 'The dear Lord told me to build him a chapel at Cross Lanes and that is why I'm doing it there.' He drew in a deep breath and some of his old spirit rose up inside of him, as he blurted out, 'If that's how they feel then I've a good mind to drop the plan altogether.'

As soon as those harsh words came out of his mouth, it was as though a dark cloud covered his mind, and he became very uneasy. Much more quietly he said, 'I'm sorry Reverend, I shouldn't have spoken in that way. The devil got hold of my spirit and I feel very ashamed of myself.'

The minister stretched out his hand and placed it on Billy's arm. 'Billy, I understand.' That was all he said. Billy realised then that the minister also felt his disappointment. With this encouragement, Billy adopted a more positive tone as he said, 'Sir, I will build the chapel, but why don't you come and see what's been achieved so far?'

They walked over the site in Cross Lanes and Billy pointed out the foundation stone and showed him where the walls would stand. The minister smiled and said, 'Billy, tonight is the night for the class meeting and I hope to be there with you all. Would you agree to allow us to cast lots to see where this new chapel ought to be built?'

At first Billy was troubled, but after a little thought, and a silent prayer, he agreed. That evening the minister took three pieces of paper which were all the same size and colour and wrote 'Twelveheads' on the first one, 'Tippets Stamps' on the second and 'Cross Lanes' on the third piece. These were all put into a hat and the minister led them in prayer, asking the Lord to show them his will for the site of the new chapel.

One of the younger men, who had no strong opinion about where the building should be, was asked to take one of the pieces of paper out of the hat. Those who favoured Twelveheads were praying that he would take out the one with that name on it, and others were eager to find out if Tippets Stamps would be drawn out.

While this was going on, Billy had moved away from the main group and was sitting in a quiet place. He was working out how to put the chapel walls up when the minister called out to him, 'Billy, our friend here has drawn out the piece of paper that has Cross Lanes on it.' He then turned to the class meeting, 'So friends,' he said, 'let us have no more disagreement about the site of the new chapel. Let's all spend as much time as we can helping our friend to get this job finished.'

Billy looked up to see how the men were reacting to this suggestion. Straight away, several of them called out, 'I'll help Billy to put the stones up.' Others said, 'Billy can count on me too.'

The next day he was to work on the afternoon shift, so almost as soon as it was light he was working at the site. No one else was there, even though they had promised to help him.

He heard a sound and then saw one of the men walking towards him, but he frowned as he noticed he was not carrying any tools. He soon discovered the reason. The man looked rather solemn and in a quiet voice said, 'I'm sorry but none of us are going to help you because we don't think the chapel should be built here.'

Before Billy could say anything, the man turned and rushed away.

'Well, Lord,' said Billy, 'I was working here on my own before the vote last night and it seems that I'll be doing the same again.' Then he added, 'But I know you are with me and you have promised to help me.'

Encouraged and Anxious

Billy had collected enough money to employ some stone masons who were experts in building walls. They wasted no time in hauling some very large stones on to the field. Then they cut them in such a way that they slotted into each other. These they then began to build up to make the first walls of the chapel.

Billy helped with the unskilled parts of the work and while he was doing so, he prayed hard because he knew he did not have enough money to pay the men the full amount. Others may have been content to let workmen wait for their cash, but Billy did not like to owe money to anyone. He was wondering whether he should ask the stonemasons to stop work after they had laid a few courses. They could then come back again when he had more in the chapel fund.

While he prayed about this, he heard the voices of some of his friends who had come to see how the chapel was progressing. However, they did not just come to watch; they had arrived with money for the work. Billy was overjoyed at these further signs of the Lord's blessing on the project. Their gifts meant that by the time the walls were finished, there would be enough money to pay the masons in full.

'What can we do?' said his new friends. 'Well,' said Billy. 'I've got enough timber to start on the roof, so you can help me saw these pieces to the correct size and then fix them in place.' Because he had those extra hands to help him, the framework of the building began to take shape.

As it was nearly midday, Billy would soon have to leave for his afternoon shift at the mine. While he was packing his tools, someone said, 'Billy, you'll need a good strong piece of timber for the main beam to run along the top of the roof.'

He knew that would be the next problem, but he called out, 'That will have to wait until I have enough money to buy it.' Immediately a strong spirit of prayer fell on him and his arms shot up in the air. He called out, in a very loud voice, 'Lord, you know that we need to get the roof finished, but it will cost a lot of money to buy a good strong piece of timber for that job. Please send your aid again and help us achieve the next bit.'

There was a loud, 'Amen,' from the men who had been helping him. Billy thanked them for the money they had brought and then hurried to his shift at the mine.

It was not long before he was hacking away at the rock many feet below ground. As he worked, he kept up a steady stream of chatter. The men liked working with him because he amused them, but he also challenged them about their spiritual needs. In each short break he would pray with those who had problems, but also ask the Lord for the money that was needed to buy the timber for the new chapel.

During a break, one of his mates said, 'Billy, where are you going to get that kind of money? It'll take at least a pound to buy a strong piece of timber.' All that Billy said in return was, 'The Lord will provide, just as he always does if we obey him.'

He arrived home exhausted, but after a night's sleep he set out again for the new chapel. He knew he did not have money to buy the wood, but there was always plenty of ground to clear of stones in the meantime.

At the same moment that Billy started to walk to his chapel, a local preacher from the Methodist church at Twelveheads was on his knees. He prayed for the people and the needs of the Methodist congregations where he preached, but while he was praying a very strange thing happened. God convicted him to go down to William Bray and give him a pound note. This troubled him because he knew that Billy was a rather strange man and, in any case, he did not belong to his own Methodist church. Nevertheless, the Lord kept prompting him to do this, so the preacher knew he had to obey. He quickly finished his breakfast and then set out for Bethel Chapel.

'Good morning, Mr Bray,' said the local preacher. This made Billy look up and he was surprised when he heard a rather gruff voice say, 'What do you want a pound note for?' Billy recognised the speaker and was surprised that he had come with money. He quickly answered, 'To buy timber to put up the main beam on that end of the chapel.'

As Billy said this, the preacher relaxed. In a more friendly tone he said, 'Do you know Billy; I've never, ever experienced such a thing in my life before. I was on my knees praying to the Lord and thinking about the Methodist Chapels, but it kept on coming into my mind, "Go and give William Bray a pound note," so here it is for you.' Billy smiled. Once again he knew the Lord was at work. After thanking the preacher, Billy took the pound note and started on the six mile walk to Truro. When he arrived at the builder's yard he found just the right sized piece. He hoisted it on to his shoulders and then walked the six miles back again to Bethel.

As little Billy was walking along the track with his very large piece of wood on his shoulder, many people came out of their houses to see him. They asked Billy what he was doing. 'This is for the new chapel,' said Billy. 'Its walls are going to ring out with the gospel, and many lost souls are going to find the Lord Jesus Christ as their Saviour and Friend.'

Suddenly a man came running out from one of the cottages and slipped a shilling into his pocket. 'Billy, this is for the new chapel.' Further down the pathway he passed a number of homes belonging to wealthy people and remembered what Joey had told him about these large houses.

She had said, 'If you ask for money at those big houses I hope you remember your manners. Make sure you go to the tradesmen's entrance.' She had explained that they were only poor working people and should remember their place in society. The front door was only for rich guests. The tradesmen's entrance was for all the ordinary people. Billy had drawn himself up to his full height, he was not very tall, and said, 'I am the son of a King and princes do not go to the back doors of homes.' Joey had been horrified and warned him that if he behaved like that, then the rich people would think he was very rude.

Despite the warnings that his wife had given him, Billy was so sure he was doing God's work knocking on the front doors of several of the houses and asking for money for his new meeting place. Some of the owners said they were loyal members of the Church of England and did not approve of people building their own chapels. However, a few gave him several shillings so that when he arrived back at Bethel Chapel, he had his beam and also two pounds that he had collected during his journey. He would then be able to buy some more timber for the roof.

Billy felt uplifted and full of joy as he walked home at the end of the day. His voice, singing loud praises to God, could be heard by many, and it cheered them up too! Everything was proceeding wonderfully. The chapel was beginning to take shape and he knew that soon many people would be able to worship the Lord at Bethel.

'You sound happy' said a voice from a cottage along the pathway. 'Yes, I am happy because the Lord has done great things for my soul, my friend.' Billy then urged the speaker to seek the Lord while he could be found. He was content because the chapel was almost finished; he was even happier because the Lord had given him a further sign of his blessing. Those two pounds would be a big help in buying what was needed to finish the roof. It might even pay for some of the floor to be covered with sand.

Little did he know that a time of great anxiety and challenge was ahead of him.

The Child Will Die

As Billy neared his cottage he saw Joey was waiting for him. He could tell that something was wrong and ran towards her shouting out, 'Whatever's the matter, dearest?' Immediately she burst into tears, 'Grace is very poorly and I fear she's going to die.'

In those days, only the very wealthy people had enough money to send for a doctor. Most families were large, but even in the richest home a number of children died very young.

Billy knew that only prayer, mixed with a great deal of love, could help young Grace. Billy rushed into the room and saw her lying in the window seat. She was very pale. Kneeling down, he stroked her head, but she had no strength to smile or even move. Billy gently placed his arms around Joey's shoulder and called the other children towards him. Then in a quiet voice he prayed to the Lord that he would have mercy upon them and heal his little Grace.

That evening he was too upset to eat any dinner. He stood over his daughter and wondered what he could do to help her. Soon the time came for him to put on his working clothes in readiness for his shift at the mine. It was then that Billy looked at the two pounds in his hand and wondered how he would pay for Grace's funeral. He knew that it would cost a pound and that meant that he would only have one left. Then the devil said to him, 'Billy, that money was given for the work of the chapel. You can't use it to pay for your daughter's funeral.'

As he walked to the mine, he talked the whole matter over with the Lord. He realised that he had put all of his spare money into the chapel fund. He knew it was God's money and so all he had to do was to get the Lord's permission to spend it. He felt that the Lord would not mind if he used it to pay for Grace's funeral.

Throughout his shift, Billy prayed about the money. He was anxious about Grace. He had seen many other children die so he was almost certain that she would not survive. This would mean that one pound of the chapel fund would be used to bury her.

With all these thoughts running around in his mind, he started to walk home at the end of the shift. As soon as he stepped out into the open air, his troubled mind was filled with light. He was still worried about Grace, but he realised the Lord was speaking to his heart. 'Well done, Billy. You are a good and faithful servant.[1] You will be rewarded for all your hard work.' Before he could say, 'Thank you Lord,' the voice spoke again, 'Yes, because you have built this chapel, I will save the child's life.' Before the devil had any time to raise doubts in Billy's mind, the Lord spoke again through his Word and said, 'I am the God of Abraham, Isaac and Jacob. Don't be doubtful. I am the Lord.'

Billy felt much happier as he opened his cottage door. 'Darling, the Lord has told me that Grace will

[1] See Matthew 25:23

live.' Joey frowned and whispered, 'you mustn't say that, Billy. It's a false hope. Grace is no better and the neighbours say she will die.' He did not wish to contradict his wife, but he assured her that the Lord had spoken very clearly to him about her recovery.

The next morning the little one was no better. He continued to pray for her as he set off for the mine once again. All during his shift he could not stop thinking of Grace. When he arrived back home again the situation was no better. The little girl had eaten nothing. The next morning she was even worse. He spent the morning working at the chapel and when he returned home there was no sign of improvement.

After dinner, Billy got ready for his afternoon shift and then, following his usual custom, he gathered all the children around him and, with Joey, he prayed earnestly for the hours that were ahead. In his prayer he said, 'Lord you told me that my child will live, but she has not eaten anything for a long time.'

He went over to the window seat to kiss his little one 'goodbye' and as he did so she stirred. He bent to hear what she was saying, 'I'm hungry, daddy.' Immediately he called 'Joey, come here quickly and bring some food. Our little darling has revived.'

From that moment onwards Grace became stronger each day and soon she was fit and well.

Once again the devil was proved to be a liar.[2] Billy did not need to take the pound meant for the chapel, because there was no funeral.

However, he still needed seven more pounds to complete the work.

---

[2] See John 8:44

Bethel Chapel Completed

Every spare penny that Billy earned or was given, was used to complete the building of Bethel Chapel. One day, while he was hard at work down the mine, a work-mate said to him, 'You're always taking risks, Billy. If you don't take some rest occasionally, you will become very ill and then you will be no use to anyone.'

He looked at his friend, but did not speak until he had finished eating his mouthful of Cornish pasty. In a very quiet voice he said, 'I don't take risks; I just depend on the Lord. He knows what I need and he supplies it. I keep praying, "Give me neither poverty nor riches, but give me only my daily bread."'[1]

That was how Billy lived every day. He was always in close touch with his God. Every time anyone urged him to take things easier he said, 'The Lord healed my little one when everyone said she would die, and I know that he is taking care of me too.'

Billy continued with the work of chapel building because it was God's will, but things did not always go smoothly. He often heard people say, 'He'll give up before the job's done.' When he heard this he smiled to himself and continued with his work.

---

[1] Proverbs 30:8

The time eventually arrived when the outside walls of the chapel were finished and the beams of the roof were in place. The next task was to find suitable material to cover the roof, to prevent rain from coming in. In those days, roofs were usually made from bundles of tightly packed reeds, called sheaves. Billy had heard these could be bought from a farmer, but his fields were several miles away from Cross Lanes. In those days there were no telephones, so the only way to send an order for goods was to find someone who was going in that direction and give them a note. Billy was too impatient to wait for that to happen. On his next free half day, he borrowed a horse and rode to the farm where they were on sale.

He quickly found the farmer, but discovered that it would cost him the large sum of two pounds for every hundred sheaves. This meant that he would need six pounds for the three hundred sheaves he would need to complete the roof. Instead of hesitating, he said to the farmer, 'Please send three hundred sheaves to Cross Lanes as soon as you can.' As he rode off, he shouted over his shoulder, 'And don't forget to include the spears so they can be fixed into place.'

What Billy had not told the farmer was that there were only two pounds in the Chapel Fund. But Billy was confident that his heavenly Father would provide the cash when it was needed.

A few days later, the first one hundred sheaves arrived and Billy handed over the two pounds. When he took this money out of his purse, he noticed that there were only a few shillings left. Despite this, Billy did not ask the farmer to wait until there was enough money for the remainder of the sheaves. His trust in his Lord was such that he knew the funds would be there when they were needed.

The sound of the farmer's horse had barely disappeared before another of Billy's friends arrived. In his hand he had two more pounds for the chapel!

The work had advanced so much, that it was time to send for the thatcher. Thatchers were experts in fixing reeds on to roofs of buildings. Billy felt tired, but relieved, as he sat down and waited for the thatcher to finish his work. Instead of drifting off to sleep, he began to sing at the top of his voice. By the time the craftsman was nearing the end of his work, more money had been brought, but when Billy looked in the purse there was just one pound in it. He did not approve of owing people money, but he knew that the thatcher's bill would be one pound and ten shillings. However, he was confident that God would supply his needs, but he also knew the Lord did not want his workmen and women to be lazy.

Billy stood up and then walked over to the very busy road that passed nearby. He smiled as he recognised the first person to come along. 'Friend,' he called out, 'you haven't given anything yet towards my Father's house, have you?'

The other man glared. He was not pleased to be asked for money. 'No,' he snapped. 'I haven't given you anything, and nor shall I.'

Billy looked disappointed and said, 'Friend, what will you say to the dear Lord on the great Day of Judgement, when he reminds you that you failed to support this chapel. I fear you will hear him saying, "I was hungry and you gave me nothing to eat, I was thirsty and you gave me nothing to drink. I was a stranger and you did not invite me in?"' [2]

Because the man knew his Bible, as many people did in those days, Billy's comment shocked him. Eventually, after a great deal of thought he muttered, 'I'll give you ten shillings, and not a penny more.' A slow smile spread across Billy's face as he took the money.

Now the outside of the chapel had been erected, Billy turned his attention to the inside of the building. Even though it was a very simple structure, he knew that some kind of furniture would be needed. They must have some benches and chairs and also window frames to hold the glass. While he was praying about these things, another friend arrived and said, 'Billy, I know where there's some good timber that is being sold cheaply. It would be just the thing for your new chapel.'

'That's kind of you to tell me,' said Billy, 'but the problem is that I only have a few shillings and I'll need at least another pound before I can buy anything more.'

---

[2] Matthew 25:42-43a

His friend's face burst into a huge smile. He slowly put his hand into his pocket and pulled out a one pound note. 'Here's your money, Billy. Go and buy what you need and may God bless you.'

Billy was overcome by the kindness of his friend and thanked him for his generous gift. A pound note was a large sum of money for any working man to give, but it was a sign of this brother's love for his Lord.

As Billy started to walk to the old mine, he burst into songs of praise. Everyone around there knew the sound of Billy's voice. They may not have admired its tunefulness, but his shouts of 'Glory, glory, glory' always filled their hearts with gladness.

The first thing he saw as he arrived at the old mine was the pile of wood. Before long he found some very suitable pieces and handed over the money for them. But just then Billy realised that the wood was far too heavy for him to carry back to the chapel site on his own.

He then remembered that one of his neighbours had a horse, so he walked to his house and knocked on his door. 'Friend, please may I borrow your horse and your cart?' His neighbour gave him a wary smile. 'You can have her with pleasure,' he said, 'but she's so idle that I can't get her to pull anything and certainly not the cart.' Billy was not deterred by this. He told him that he would try to encourage the animal to work. The neighbour said, 'You'll need this whip; otherwise she won't do anything.'

Billy took hold of the horse and led it to its place between the shafts of the cart. To the astonishment of its owner, the horse meekly followed Billy's leading and they got to the old mine without any trouble. The horse stood still while Billy and some men loaded all the wood on to the cart.

The horse even kept up a steady stride all the way to the chapel site.

Later that day, Billy returned the horse to its owner. The man said, 'And how much trouble did she give you once you were out of my sight?'

'None at all' said Billy. 'In fact I have never seen a better behaved horse in all my life.'

Its owner looked very puzzled. 'It has been months since she would pull a cart for me, or anyone else!'

'I'm not joking,' replied Billy. 'I've never seen a better mare in all my life. And here is the reason. Today she was working for a very strong company. That company was the Father, the Son and the Holy Spirit. All horses, angels, men – yes, and devils must obey the orders of that company. Your horse was drawing wood for my Father's house.'

Providing a pulpit or platform for the preacher to stand on was next on Billy's list. Again he had very little money and wondered where he could find the wood to build a strong pulpit. He then heard that some furniture was being sold by auction. As soon as he arrived at the sale, he noticed a large cupboard. It had been especially built to stand in the corner of a room. Immediately he realised that he could cut a slit down its back, strengthen the middle and make a place to hold the Bible. If he put some steps behind it, a suitable platform would be formed for the preacher to stand upon to deliver his sermons.

While he was looking closely at the cupboard, someone came up to him and said, 'You're Billy Bray, aren't you?' When he said he was, the man asked, 'How much do you think they will sell this for?' Billy replied, 'About six shillings, I should think.' The other man smiled at Billy and pressed some coins into his hand. 'There you are Billy. There's six shilling pieces for it.'

Billy was overjoyed at this sudden change of events, but his troubles were not yet over. He had never been to an auction before and did not realise that the man in charge would invite people to bid for each item. The normal thing was for someone to shout out a sum of money. The auctioneer would ask if anyone wanted to offer more for it and the item would be sold to the one who offered the greatest sum of money.

However, Billy was excited and he knew that the Lord wanted him to have the cupboard. When the sale opened he called out, 'Six shillings because I want it for the pulpit for the chapel I'm building.' But before he could move forward to pay the money another person shouted out a higher sum and very quickly the man in charge said, 'Sold to that man for seven shillings.'

Billy was shocked and called out, 'No mister. The price is six shillings and I've got the money right here in my hand.' Someone explained to him that he was too late because another person had bought it. He was filled with disappointment and knew that he had to give back the six shillings. He looked around, but the man who had given him the money had disappeared.

As he left the sale, he saw his cupboard disappearing up the hill on the back of a cart. He decided to follow it to see where it was going. The cart stopped outside a house and several men started to heave it off the cart and take it up to the front door. As Billy drew nearer he wondered why it was taking so long to get it inside. When he was nearer still, he could see what the problem was; it was too big for the doorway. They tried it frontwards and backwards. Then they laid it on its side to see if it would go in that way, but none of those methods worked.

As Billy started to move on past the house he heard the owner shout out, 'Seven whole shillings, all spent for nothing. All I can do is to chop it up for firewood.' As soon as Billy heard that he ran up the path and said, 'You can do better than that. If I give you six shillings will you put it back on the cart and take it down to the chapel I'm building at Cross Lanes?'

The man quickly agreed and was pleased to get some of his money back. This meant that Billy had his pulpit, and he did not have to worry about how he was going to move it from the place of the auction to Bethel Chapel.

These are just a few examples of the way in which the Lord provided for Bethel Chapel. However, Bethel wasn't the only chapel that Billy built. Within five or six years, the Lord put it into his heart to build another one and then a third. Each of these chapels rang with God's praises for many years and large numbers of people came to find the Saviour within their walls.

The Vicar of Baldhu

As the years went by, Billy was often called to go and preach in other areas of Cornwall. But eventually the day came when Billy believed God was calling him to give up working at the mines and devote all his time to preaching the gospel. Joey was concerned about how they would make ends meet.

'It's like this Joey,' Billy explained. 'God is saying, "Billy, you go and do what I am calling you to do. I am still the God who provides for his people."'

So this is what Billy did and as he became older the calls for him to preach increased a great deal. Because he was now speaking all over Cornwall, it became clear that they should leave Twelveheads and move much nearer to the centre of the county. This was how they came to move the twenty miles from his village to the large town of Bodmin.

Some years after their move to Bodmin, Billy received a letter from his brother James. He told him that trees were being cut down on Baldhu and there was talk of houses being built there. This pleased Billy, but he was even more excited when he learned that a church and a schoolroom were also planned for that spot. 'There you are, Joey. The Lord said to me that he would give me that mountain.'

Joey had no wish to dampen Billy's enthusiasm, but in a worried tone she said, 'If there is to be a church there, then the people will belong to the Church of England not to the Bible Christians. You know how some of those church people despise the rest of us.'

The Church of England used Prayer Books and their services were conducted with quiet dignity. This kind of thing did not appeal to Billy. Instead, he preferred the much simpler meetings of the Methodists and the Bible Christians. Chapel preachers did not read their prayers out of books and their hymn singing was usually very loud and exuberant.

A few months after this conversation, he had some preaching engagements in West Cornwall. He had no service to take one Sunday morning, so he walked up to the new church at Baldhu, found a pew and sat down. He thought it was very strange, because it was so solemn and quiet. Everyone stood up as the vicar, the Reverend William Haslam, proceeded slowly into the church, with little boys in dresses walking in front of him. The vicar had a very solemn expression on his face, but what horrified Billy even more was the sight of the coloured robes he was wearing. They were so different from the way Billy dressed to take services. The old black coat he had been given some years before had always been quite good enough for him.

As the liturgy started, Billy became troubled because the prayers were not personal; they were read from a book. Their language was certainly dignified, but their meaning did not reach into his soul. Everything was so 'prim and proper' and he wanted to cry out, 'The Spirit of God is not in this place.' But he didn't.

Billy left the Baldhu church feeling very sad and he hung his head as he walked towards the chapel where he was due to preach that afternoon. Over and over he said to the Lord, 'Father, how can the people of Baldhu be converted while that man is in charge?' Everything he had seen and heard troubled him, but he never forgot the Lord's promise to 'give him that mountain.'

However, Billy did not know that the Lord was already working in the Rev William Haslam's heart.

God's work first came to light when Mr Haslam's gardener, a man called John Gill, fell ill. John was not only the vicar's servant; he was also a faithful member of the Church of England. William and John had become close friends, even though they were from totally different classes of society. As soon as the vicar heard that John was unwell, he rushed to his servant's cottage. He became very upset when he heard John was suffering from a horrible lung disease that afflicted many miners at that time. There was no cure in those days and those who caught it often died a slow and agonising death.

From then onwards, Mr Haslam visited his friend every day. He read him various set prayers and comforting passages from the Bible. He took him the bread and wine of Holy Communion and informed him that he was receiving the actual body and blood of Christ. On one occasion, he looked at his friend and said, 'John, as you have been baptised in the Church of England and are a faithful member of the church, God will take you safely to heaven when the time comes for you to leave this earth.'

But despite Mr Haslam's prayers, John's condition worsened each day. He wondered why none of his prayers or the teaching of the Church had brought healing.

When he heard that John had sent for a chapel preacher to come and pray with him, Mr Haslam was even more distressed. He believed that it was only within the Church of England that true salvation could be found. No doubt the noisy preachers from the chapels would do their best to cheer up John, but no bishop had placed his hands upon them; nor had they been given authority to dispense the sacraments.

During breakfast the next morning, he shared this news with his wife. 'My dear, I understand that these rough men tell their people a great deal about hell and judgement and they say that each one of us is a sinner, even clergymen.'

His wife smiled and said, 'But doesn't the church teach that there must be judgement for sin?'

'Yes, indeed it does, but when the holy sacrament of bread and wine is administered by a priest then peace enters the soul.' William frowned and added, 'John certainly knows that, so I can't understand why he felt he should send for a dissenter?'[1] He went on to tell his wife how he had been trying to encourage John to look upwards. 'I want to encourage him, not discourage him as these men seem to want to do. I'll go and see him tomorrow and hope that I am not too late to remove their foolish ideas from his head.'

The next morning, the vicar quietly knocked on John's door. He wondered whether his friend was still alive. While he waited for someone to answer the door, he quickly thought of some suitable words of sympathy. However, he was surprised to hear a great deal of noise coming from the house. When he was invited in, he was amazed to see that John was up and dressed and walking around the room. He was shouting praises to God. 'My friend,' said the vicar, 'you are well again. What has happened to cause this miracle?'

Mr Haslam sat down, but became very uneasy when he heard John's story. 'Vicar, the chapel preacher told me that I was a lost sinner and I needed to come to Jesus just as I am. He told me that if I repented of my sin, the Lord would save me, He also said that God would heal me of my sickness.'

---

[1] 'Dissenter' was one of the names given to those Protestants who disagreed with the Church of England. They were also called Non-conformists, because they didn't conform to the Church of England services.

John looked very serious and then added, 'When I heard that, it made me very distressed because I have done some terrible things in my life, but the preacher told me that Jesus receives sinners[2] and he urged me to seek the Lord.

'Immediately I told the Lord everything that was on my heart and a wonderful peace came over me. It was as though the Lord Jesus himself spoke to me and said, "Come to me … and I will give you rest."[3]

'Vicar, do you know that straight away my coughing stopped and my breathing became easier and, as you see, I can now walk again and praise God without any wheezing.'

Mr Haslam was pleased that his friend was better, but inside he was far from happy. Since early childhood, he had placed his hope of salvation on receiving the sacraments and obeying the teaching of the Church of England. He could not understand how his friend had received peace without receiving the sacraments of the mass.

That very day, the Rev William Haslam began to enter into experiences that were beyond his thoughts and out of his control.

Two people were greatly troubled at this time. Little Billy Bray could not understand how the hill of Baldhu would ever ring to the praises of God, and the Rev William Haslam was perplexed to know how his

---

[2] See Luke 15:2

[3] See Matthew 11:28

servant had been helped by a rowdy chapel-preacher. Neither Billy nor William knew that the Holy Spirit was already working in the heart of the Vicar of Baldhu.

Then a Mr Aitkin, the Vicar of Pendeen, invited William Haslam to visit him and give advice on the new church that was to be built there.

Pendeen was a little village very near Land's End, at the south western tip of Cornwall. It was a long way but the next morning William caught the stage coach and rode as far as Penzance. Then he walked to Pendeen. As soon as he reached his destination, William was warmly welcomed by Mr Aitkin. Soon they were sitting in front of a welcoming, large fire. 'How are things going with your parish at Baldhu, friend?' asked his host.

'I'm not satisfied,' said Mr Haslam. 'Many of these Cornish people do not like following the dignified services of the Church of England. They just want to sing the words to rowdy tunes.' Then he told his host how anxious he was because his gardener had become involved with some chapel people. He could not understand why they had been the instrument in his friend's healing.

William could not believe his ears when his host said, 'If I was taken ill, I would certainly not send for you.'

William responded with an angry tone, 'And why is that?'

Not only was he alarmed with Mr Aitkin's answer; he was shocked when he heard Mr Aitkin's reason, 'It's because you aren't converted.'

It would have been too rude to walk out of the room, so he sat in annoyed silence. Mr Aitkin continued, 'If you were truly the Lord's, then you would not be sitting here complaining about the healing of your gardener; you would be standing there with him and praising God for his gracious kindness.'

For many hours they sat in front of the fire and discussed the teaching of the Bible. Mr Aitkin had made him think, when he said, 'From reading your Bible you know about the water of life that Jesus spoke of. But, my friend, do you know whether you have this stream springing up inside you?'

Eventually, William was shown to his bedroom, but he could not sleep because the words of his host kept buzzing around in his mind. 'Do you have this living water springing up inside of you?'[4]

When he finally arrived back in Baldhu, he told his wife about his uneasy time in Pendeen. 'Do you know, my dear, Mr Aitkin asked me when I knew the peace of God in my soul.'

'What did you tell him, my sweet one?'

Mr Haslam looked smugly at his wife and said, 'I told him that was my experience every time I celebrated the Holy Communion service.'

Mrs Haslam looked at him very gently and said, 'But William, how long does that peace last?'

Her question startled him because it was the same one that Mr Aitkin had asked. William tried to look

---

[4] See John 4:10-14

kindly at his wife as he said, 'It lasts almost until the next time that I consecrate the elements.'

The next few days were troubled times for the Vicar of Baldhu. When Sunday came he felt too unwell to face the people. However, he knew his duty and forced himself to go to church. He decided that he would only read the service from the Prayer Book and then go home again to lie down. He had already asked the church clerk to select the hymns for the service so that would be one less thing to worry about.

Although he intended only to stay for a short while he felt he should say a few words about the Gospel passage that had been set for that day.

He climbed up into the pulpit deep in thought. Then he gave out as his text, 'What do you think about the Christ?'[5] He explained that the Pharisees and scribes did not know that Jesus was the Son of God, or that he had come to save them. As he spoke about this subject, its meaning began to flow into his mind. He paused, leaned forward on the pulpit and then looked straight at the people. To his surprise his voice rose and he shouted out, 'You are no better than the Pharisees yourselves. You do not believe that he is the Son of God and that he has come to save you, anymore than they did.'

The words then flowed rapidly into his mind and out again through his mouth. He had never experienced such things before. He was animated as

5 Matthew 22:42

he spoke about the message of salvation. Suddenly a wonderful light and rich joy began to fill his whole being. For the first time in his life he saw what the Pharisees had failed to see.

Every eye looked at him and all ears strained to catch each syllable that fell from his lips. Suddenly there was a commotion in the congregation as a man stood up and shouted, 'The parson's been converted! The parson is saved! Hallelujah.' Instead of someone telling him to be quiet, other people joined him until the whole congregation were caught up with praises to God.

When the place again became quiet, there was a sound of gentle sobbing and about twenty people were heard calling out to the Lord to have mercy on their souls. No one left the church that day before they had found the same peace that now resided within their vicar.

News of such tremendous events could not be kept quiet for long, but not everyone was happy. Mr Haslam's own schoolmaster was furious when he heard what had happened. He had always joined with his vicar in condemning 'The brash Methodists and Bible Christians'. A number of other members of the congregation joined with the schoolmaster in complaint about their vicar's behaviour.

However, none of this rising opposition deterred William Haslam. He was filled with praise to God and overcome with joy, when one of the first people to rush towards him at the end of that service was his dear gardener. He and John had started off their relationship as employer and employee. Then they became friends, but now they were brothers in Christ.

From that day forward every service at the Baldhu church was filled with loud praises to God, who has mercy on those who call upon him.

A few weeks later, William and his wife were sitting in their dining room having a leisurely breakfast, when they heard footsteps in the hall and someone shouting, 'Praise the Lord. Praise the Lord.' The vicar hurried to the door. When he opened it, he saw a small happy-looking man wearing a coarse black coat that was several sizes too big for him.

'Well, my friend,' said William, 'who may you be?'

'I'm Billy Bray,' said the visitor with a twinkle in his eyes, 'and are you the parson?' When William explained that he was, Billy said, 'I hear that you are converted. Is that so?'

'Yes, thank God,' replied William.

Before William could ask him inside, Billy peered into the room and asked, 'Is your wife saved?'

As soon as Billy had been assured that she was, he walked into the dining room and bowed low towards Mrs Haslam. Then he turned to the Vicar again, 'Do you have any servants?'

Mr Haslam explained that there were several and they were in the kitchen about their work.

'Are they converted too?' asked Billy.

As soon as William explained that everyone had been saved, Billy disappeared into the room beyond and the vicar and his wife soon heard loud sounds of praises to God filling the kitchen.

Billy eventually came back into the dining room, but before Mr Haslam could invite him to sit and eat breakfast with them, Billy ran towards the vicar, took him up into his arms and danced around the room with him, singing the praises of God.

Billy finally sat down and began to eat. He told his hosts that twenty years earlier, God had told him that he would give him the people who lived on this mountain. He mentioned how he had come to the church some months before. 'But you know, sir, it was without my Father God's permission and I went away disappointed because the gospel of salvation wasn't being preached here.'

The vicar and his wife looked bemused when Billy continued, 'Then at half past eleven last night Father God spoke to me again and I felt called to go to Baldhu.'

Billy did not wait until the morning, but put on his clothes, hitched a donkey up to the only cart he could find – which happened to be a very slow one – and he had come straight to the vicarage.

It was a very long breakfast time, but everyone in the house, including Billy, were overflowing with joy and blessing because of the Lord's gracious goodness to them all.

Billy turned to the vicar and said, 'I've got something to ask you sir.'

'Will you preach in one of the chapels for me?' Billy asked tentatively. A slight frown began to crease William Haslam's forehead. 'This request you have made of me, Billy, makes things rather difficult because I have only ever preached in the Church of England. I have always believed that Methodist and Bible Christian Chapels are not true places of worship.'

After a long pause, a huge smile shot around his face. He had resolved the conflict within him. Looking at Billy he said, 'My dear friend, Billy. It would give me the greatest of pleasure to come and preach in one of your chapels and join with your people in singing praises to our glorious God.'

And so it was, that soon after that date the Rev William Haslam, Vicar of the Church at Baldhu, stood up in the pulpit of the nearby Bible Christian Chapel. On the first occasion he preached, Brother William felt an extraordinary and glorious elation and his words flowed freely with the power of the Holy Spirit. At the end of the service, many people were in tears and others were crying out to the Lord to have mercy on their souls.

After that, Mr Haslam not only preached in Billy's chapels, he also joined him in open air missions around the southern part of Cornwall. In fact the whole of his life was changed and Baldhu church became a place where huge numbers flocked to hear the preaching of the gospel. As a result, many came to know the Lord Jesus as their Saviour and Friend.

Billy continued to preach throughout Cornwall and many found forgiveness for their sins. Billy had much to thank God for.

Naturally Billy was very sad when one of his children died, but he still praised the Lord. Then the bitterest blow fell one day in 1864; his dear wife, Joey, also went to heaven.

Billy lived another three and a half years after that, but his strenuous life had by then begun to take its toll. He gradually became weaker and was finally unable to travel very far from his home. However, his spirits never flagged despite his inability to climb up into a pulpit anymore. He was not afraid to die and in his final year on earth he told a number of people, 'I shall be in my Father's house soon.'

One day he was so unwell that he finally agreed to send for a doctor. Although he was very weak, his mind was still very active. As he lay on his bed, he looked up at the physician and said, 'Now, doctor, I have sent for you because people say you are an honest man. I understand that you tell your patients the truth about their condition.' After the doctor had examined him, Billy said, 'Well, doctor, how is it?'

The doctor looked grave and said, 'You wanted to know the truth, Mr Bray, so I will tell you. You are going to die before very long.' When Billy heard this news he shouted out, 'Glory! Glory be to God! I shall soon be in heaven!' Then he looked at the doctor and in a much more serious tone said, 'Shall I give them your compliments, doctor, and tell them that you will be following me to heaven one day?'

The doctor was startled by Billy's question and he left the house in a very thoughtful mood. So we see, that even at the very end of his very full life, Billy never lost an opportunity to challenge people about their relationship with the Lord Jesus. He knew that this is the most important thing in anyone's life.

His whole being had been transformed when the Lord came into his life and he was made a child of God. If Billy Bray was alive today he would ask you, who are reading this book right now, 'Are you right with God? Do you know the Lord Jesus Christ as your own personal Saviour and Friend?'

Billy and Joey had moved back to their home village of Twelveheads a few years before Joey's death. After his funeral, Billy's body was buried in the churchyard of his friend, the Vicar of Baldhu. Sadly, that church is no longer in use as a place of worship. It has been converted into living accommodation. However, the graveyard, including Billy's plot and gravestone is still there and anyone may visit it. The sign on the gate of the church yard says, 'Billy Bray Memorial. Visitors Welcome. 10.30 a.m. to 4.30 p.m.'

Billy's tombstone reads, 'In memory of William, better known as Billy Bray, who died at Twelveheads 25th May 1868, Aged 73 years.' In front of this inscription is a simple flower vase with the words, 'Dear Billy' engraved in it.

Billy Bray Timeline

1794	Billy Bray born on 1st June.
	U.S. Congress changes U.S.A. flag to 15 stars and stripes.
1800	Washington D.C. becomes U.S.A. Capital.
1801	Billy Bray's dad dies.
1801	The Kingdom of Great Britain and the Kingdom of Ireland merge to form the United Kingdom.
1804	Napoleon crowns himself Emperor of France.
1805	Battle of Trafalgar.
1807	Highland Clearances begin.
1811	Billy leaves Cornwall for work.
1812	America at war with Britain and Canada.
1814	The first steam locomotive invented by George Stephenson.
1815	Britain's first Primary School is opened.
	Wellington defeats Napoleon at Waterloo.
1818	Billy returns to Cornwall.
1821	Billy marries Joanna (Joey) Bray.
1822	Caledonian Canal opened.
1823	Billy reads John Bunyan's book and becomes a Christian.

1824	Billy begins to preach.
1825	The first train travels from Stockton to Darlington.
1827	John Walker invents modern matches.
1830	French Revolution.
1833	The Slavery Abolition Act bans slavery across the British empire.
1838	Queen Victoria is crowned.
1843	Thames Tunnel completed.
	Disruption of the Church of Scotland.
1851	Isaac Singer invents the sewing machine.
1854-56	The Crimean War.
1859	First American oil well drilled in Pennsylvania.
1860	Abraham Lincoln elected 16th President of America.
1862	Alexander Parkes invents the first man-made plastic.
1864	Joey dies.
1868	Billy dies.
1877	Billy's biography published.

From the Author

Billy Bray was a man who was constantly driven by the Holy Spirit. He spoke out boldly for the Lord and was not worried by the consequences.

He was born on 27th January, 1794 in the small village of Twelveheads in west Cornwall and died seventy-three years later on 25th May, 1868. In his early days there were few proper roads and the workers' cottages were warmed by open wood fires. The only lighting was by candles or oil lamps. Most people had to walk everywhere, because they were too poor to own a pony and trap and the railways did not reach Cornwall until about 1838.

Although Billy died over 100 years ago, many stories are still told about him in western Cornwall. Almost everything we know about his life comes from his own Journal and a book called *The King's Son*. This is a biography which was first published in 1877 by the Rev F. W. Bourne. When Mr Bourne was a young minister, he met Billy who by that time was a very old man. Mr Bourne's book has gone through many editions; the one I have been using was issued in 1902.

More recently, a few other books have been written about Billy's life, but they have all been based on earlier ones. In 2004 Chris Wright published a book called *Billy Bray in his own words*. This is a very thorough investigation of published material, church records and stories still circulating about Billy's life.

Mr Wright worked very hard to discover which of these many stories are based on fact, and not just 'folk-lore'. His book has been invaluable to me as I have tried to give to you a flavour of Billy Bray's life and work.

We do not know the names of all of Billy's children and almost nothing about their lives. This means I have had to use my imagination a great deal in trying to give you some idea of what life was like in those far off days. Where possible, I have used conversations that we know took place, but I have modernised the wording and removed the Cornish dialect.

Even though I have invented several parts of this story, I have based these on known incidents in Billy's life. I have tried to recreate the spirit of bygone Cornwall, as I have told you something about our hero and his work for the Lord.

I am very thankful to so many who have helped me in my research of Billy's life. I am especially grateful to Jamie Craze, of Feock, Cornwall who took me to the Three Eyes Chapel and other places associated with Billy's life, and also to Rev Barry Buckingham, a Cornish man who now lives in Bracknell, Berkshire.

Michael Bentley, July 2011

Thinking Further Topics

1. Imagine that you are living in a Cornish village in the 1800s. How would your house be different? How would work be different? How would you be different yourself? Billy Bray changed from being one person to being something quite different. What were the noticeable changes in his life and why did they happen?

   Have there ever been any big changes in your life? What brought those about? Can you think of changes that you need in your life? Why can it be hard to change and why are some people so afraid of it?

2. Billy had a problem with alcohol before he became a Christian. What bad things happened because of this? Was it just Billy who suffered? Have you ever seen someone do something that hurts their life and the life of their friends?

   Alcohol is just as addictive as it always was and has destroyed many people's homes and families. At one point in the book, Billy realises that, now he is a Christian, he is taking home a lot more money than he used to. Can you think of other ways his family life improved when he repented of his sin and turned his life over to God?

3. This book is about Billy Bray, but it equally could be a book about Joey, his wife. How is Joey a good

example to us of how to live our lives – but how was she not a good example? In the book it says that Joey's parents approved of Billy. Do you think they really knew what sort of man he was? Joey didn't blame Billy for the fact that she had drifted away from God, as she knew it had started long before she met him.

Was there a time in your life when you were closer to God than you are now? Are you letting other people influence you in a wrong way? In what ways do the lives of others diminish our love for God, and tempt us away from godly living?

4. Billy Bray, once he was converted, was well known for his happiness and his rather bad, but joyful singing. How would you describe someone who was truly happy? Can you make yourself truly happy? From what Billy Bray said, what was the secret of his happiness?

Some people say that there is a difference between the words happiness and joy. Do you think that's true? At one point in the book, Mr Haslam said to his wife that he had peace, but it wasn't the peace of God as it wasn't a peace that lasted. If you wanted to describe what it was like to feel really and truly at peace how would you do that?

5. Billy liked to use plain and simple words when he preached. Find a Bible story about Jesus and

imagine that you are teaching it to someone who can't read or speak English very well. How would you explain the story to them? What are the most important things someone needs to know about Jesus and how would you bring these out in the story?

6. Billy was enthusiastic about Jesus. He had discovered the wonderful truth of salvation and had real peace at last. He wanted to tell everyone. He shouted and sang and danced in his excitement about the gospel. Do you sometimes feel really excited about God? Do you tell others about it or do you keep it to yourself?

   Do you remember in the story, when the Vicar of Baldhu came back from visiting his friend, something amazing happened. Why is it strange that he was converted? What might you assume about a vicar and his relationship with God?

7. Throughout the story of Billy Bray, you read lots of Bible verses and hymns. They were a great help to Billy Bray when he first started as a Christian. Write down a Bible verse or a hymn that is special to you. Why do you find it helpful? How has God used his Word in the past to strengthen you?

   Find a Bible dictionary or go to the website www.biblegateway.com and look up different verses on some of the following themes: Help, Deliverance, Protection, Love, Forgiveness, Peace.

8. Billy lived in a really exciting time in history. Look at the timeline and you will see famous battles, inventions, and well known names from the 1800s. But Billy was focused on saving souls. Think about the future. What is happening in our world at the moment that will be in the history books in years to come? What is happening that we will all have forgotten about in a few years time? Think about the truth of God. How is that more important than anything?

MORE IN THE TRAILBLAZER SERIES

The Adventures Series
An ideal series to collect

Have you ever wanted to visit the rainforest? Have you ever longed to sail down the Amazon river? Would you just love to go on Safari in Africa? Well these books can help you imagine that you are actually there.

Pioneer missionaries retell their amazing adventures and encounters with animals and nature. In the Amazon you will discover tree frogs, piranha fish and electric eels. In the Rainforest you will be amazed at the armadillo and the toucan. In the blistering heat of the African Savannah you will come across lions and elephants and hyenas. And you will discover how God is at work in these amazing environments.

Rocky Mountain Adventures by Betty Swinford
ISBN 978-1-85792-962-1

African Adventures by Dick Anderson
ISBN 978-1-85792-807-5

Amazon Adventures by Horace Banner
ISBN 978-1-85792-440-4

Cambodian Adventures by Donna Vann
ISBN 978-1-84550-474-8

Great Barrier Reef Adventures by Jim Cromarty
ISBN 978-1-84550-068-9

Himalayan Adventures by Penny Reeve
ISBN 978-1-84550-080-1

Kiwi Adventures by Bartha Hill
ISBN 978-1-84550-282-9

New York City Adventures by Donna Vann
ISBN 978-1-84550-546-2

Outback Adventures by Jim Cromarty
ISBN 978-1-85792-974-4

Pacific Adventures by Jim Cromarty
ISBN 978-1-84550-475-5

Rainforest Adventures by Horace Banner
ISBN 978-1-85792-627-9

Rocky Mountain Adventures by Betty Swinford
ISBN 978-1-85792-962-1

Scottish Highland Adventures by
Catherine Mackenzie
ISBN 978-1-84550-281-2

Wild West Adventures by Donna Vann
ISBN 978-1-84550-065-8

CHRISTIAN FOCUS PUBLICATIONS

Christian Focus | Christian Heritage | CF4K | Mentor

Christian Focus Publications publishes books for adults and children under its four main imprints: Christian Focus, CF4K, Mentor and Christian Heritage. Our books reflect that God's word is reliable and Jesus is the way to know him, and live for ever with him.

Our children's publication list includes a Sunday School curriculum that covers pre-school to early teens; puzzle and activity books. We also publish personal and family devotional titles, biographies and inspirational stories that children will love.

If you are looking for quality Bible teaching for children then we have an excellent range of Bible story and age specific theological books.

From pre-school to teenage fiction, we have it covered!

Find us at our web page:
www.christianfocus.com

CF4 •K
Because you're never too young to know Jesus